Vintage Sewing Accessories

Red and white all over was a popular theme in the past, and continues to be popular.

Potholder

This bright Flower Garden potholder will cheer up anyone's kitchen. It is reminiscent of the cozy quilts found in many homes not so long ago.
Patterns on page 28.

Dolly Yarn Holder

Cleverly designed, this cute little polka dot dolly is wearing a sassy bonnet while she keeps your yarn safe from inquisitive kittens and small children.
Patterns on page 25.

Clown Bean Bag

Is he a doll or a toy? He's both. This perky little clown is a bean bag and he's just waiting to play with you. His clothes and hat are made of happy red polka dots; his eyes and nose are dots, too.
Patterns on pages 20-21.

Pincushion Chair

Don't lean back on this chair; it's a pincushion! Open the seat and you'll find a secret compartment for other sewing treasures. A decorative crochet edging sets off the back and sides of this adorable sewing room accessory.
Patterns on pages 22-24.

Pantaloon Potholder

Clever, vintage potholders made with polka dot fabric scraps were both useful and decorative. These potholders were quite a bit smaller than those we see and use today; however, this makes them more attractive. Antique potholders are quite sought after as textile collectibles and are worth big dollars for such small items.
Patterns on page 26.

Sunbonnet Needlecase

Polka dots for the "home" include precious sewing accessories like this Sunbonnet needlecase made in the 1940's. Open the polka dot bonnet and you'll find needles and pins.
Patterns on pages 26-27.

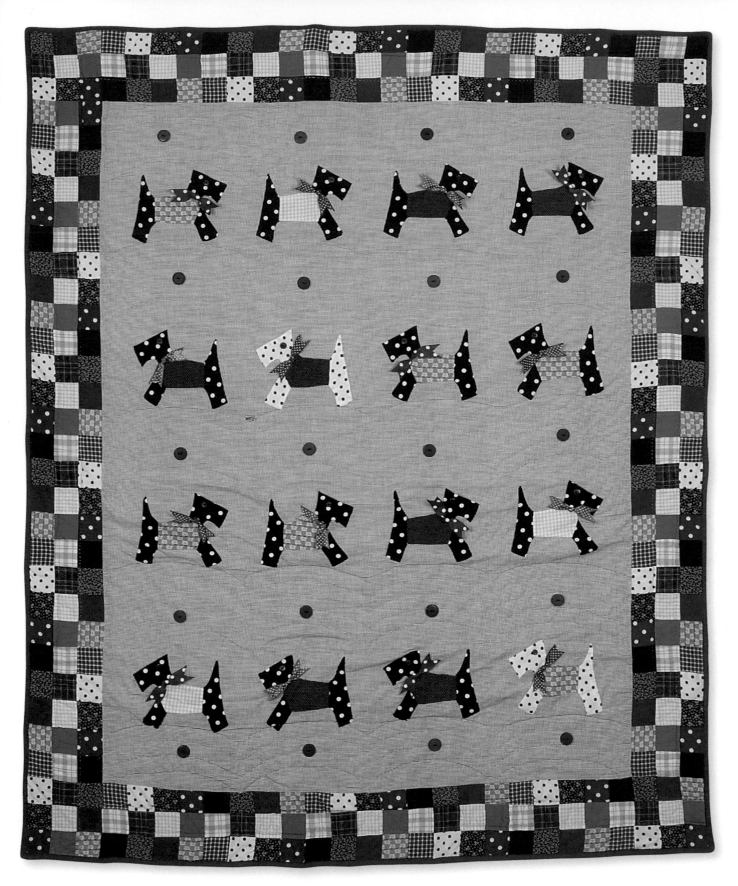

Scottie Dogs Quilt

Dots and plaid, buttons and bows; what could be more appropriate for a quilt full of Scotties? They're all decked out in their Sunday best. Is it a parade? Two of the dogs are white, obvious throwbacks from a previous generation! Wouldn't you just love for these polka dot pups to romp and play? Create this quilt for your favorite child or grandchild.

Patterns on page 55.

Needlework Quilt

This bright Red and White quilt is especially clever because the Red checks are made of polka dotted and checkered fabric while the White checks are embroidered with the sewing implements of the day. The border is created with Red dot scallops, which are really half dots, that become hearts when they meet the checks at the four corners.
Patterns on pages 52-54.

Nancy's Needlecase

This heart-shaped, open-fold needlecase is charming in dots, accented with a polka dot button. You'll want to make several to give to friends just to let them know you are thinking of them.
Patterns on page 44.

"Sewing circles of old" often made small tokens of appreciation for family and friends and, yet, made them useful to the "duties of the day."

Polka Dots

In June of 1931, Ladies Home Journal showed garments in many styles, all in polka dots. In 1939, a full-length gown pattern was promoted as the latest for that year's parties. Feed sacks of the "depression era" showed polka dots in many colors. They turned into clever useful items like pajamas and aprons. Patterns designed for feed sacks often showed the dot bags being used.

The 1940's designated the "polka dot" as a Spring Classic pattern according to the Sears Roebuck catalog. Montgomery Ward catalogs showed pretty blouses, suits and dresses in polka dots of all sizes. Large buttons were used frequently for embellishment. Dots were used with many other designs such as floral strips. Drab colors were prevalent.

A 1940's printed cut-out of a purple polka dot apron preceded a 1950's half apron cut-out with green polka dots and black poodles.

The happy 1950's, a more carefree era, gave us red and white kitchens across America. They were followed closely by red and white polka dot curtains, aprons, housedresses and even glassware.

Minnie Mouse, Little Red Riding Hood and many a clown sported polka dots in their attire. A Spiegel catalog in 1950, referred to a dainty red polka dot dress as a "year-round favorite." It came in red and white or navy and white for only $2.98. Home Arts needlecraft magazine talked about using dot chenille.

The 1960's and 70's were rebellious and outrageous in many aspects, especially fashion. Polka dots became "mod" in bold colors. Sears was selling Arnel triacetate jersey in delicious colors, "right on the dot" according to the page selling three styles of polka dot dresses for under $10.98 each. Teenagers readily responded to the polka dot tapered blouses, perfect for jeans. A cotton duck "scooter skirt," from many clothing manufacturers, also, became a hit.

Dots became calmer in the 1980's. They were reused in a big way as the quilting industry exploded. "Pin dots" were printed on cotton in every shade and tint, as they replaced solid colors previously used for quilting and crafts. Dots, however, took more of a back seat in the fashion industry during this time.

Dot Pizzaz

Smart, energetic and lively. Polka dots are all of these things. Wherever they're found, things get a little more exciting. Want to liven up a room? Add dots. They have a way of making you smile, and as everyone knows, smiling is good for you... a smiley face is really a dot!

Country Girl

This pretty young miss, all dressed in polka dots and ruffles, has her hands full with chickens and ducks. And everyone knows guinea fowl wouldn't be seen in anything but dots. Patterns on page 57.

Floral Towel

Bring a little sunshine into your kitchen with this cheery little towel. It sports daisy-like flowers and bright blue fruit. Border it with dots and daydream your blues away. Patterns on page 56.

Dancing Plates

Cheer up the kitchen; get in the mood. You'll smile back at these colorful plates as they sprout legs and arms to dance merrily around, decked out in blue and white polka dots. Patterns on page 58

Boy Meets Girl

A "How do you do?" in polka dots. That would get any relationship off to a good start. The girl and boy, dressed in dots and surrounded by flowers would be a happy addition to any home. Patterns on pages 60-61.

Blue Basket

This basket is overflowing with pink and purple flowers just waiting to cheer up you or a special friend. Dots surround the flowers and they are themselves big bright dots. Patterns on pages 62-63.

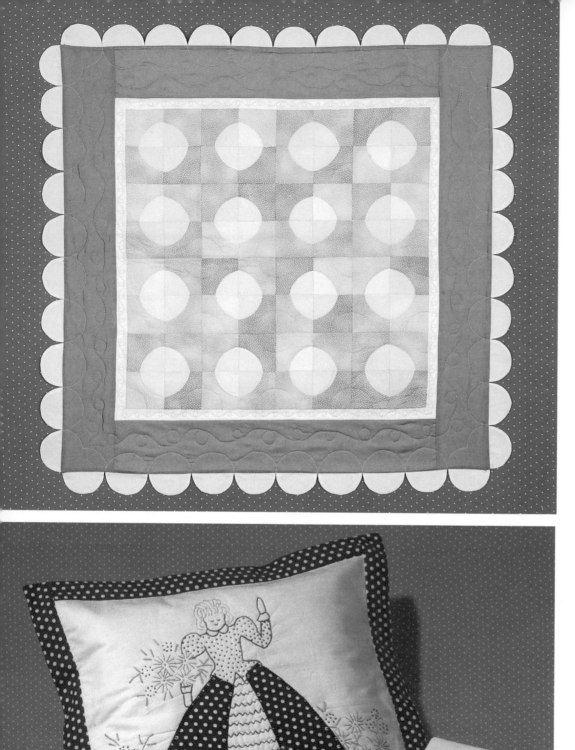

Dots in Pink

Since the beginning of time people have decorated their homes. The quilt, pillow, tablecloth, and towel on this page all did their part to make this happen. Add that special touch to your home with dots.

Ann's Dots Quilt

This pretty quilt features polka dots on several different background colors with their shape repeated in the circular quilt pattern and the scalloped edging. Patterns on page 69.

Pink Lady Pillow

The pretty lady reflects our fascination with times past. Embroidery is used along with an applique skirt. The dots, on a bright pink field, are also used as trim around the pillow. Patterns on page 66.

Dancing Ladies

The dancing ladies on this playful tablecloth are embroidered but their colorful dresses are appliqued with modified polka dots on a plaid background. The round dots become flowers which are repeated as cheerfull embroidered flowers sprouting from the hill on which they dance. Patterns on page 64.

Pink Peach Towel

This tea towel of homespun cotton is embellished with a white dot on pink fabric and the leaves with white dots on green. Both leaves and fruit are accented with embroidery. Patterns on page 90.

Favorite Animals Quilt

Whether it flies, swims or is just plain cute, your favorite animal might be found on this cuddly quilt.

The bright colors invite you in and the irresistible animals beg you to play. Purple elephants and blue cats, red chickens and pink bunnies; throw out all the rules and just be creative.

Sew your heart right into it and you have a perfect gift for a child or for a friend.

Patterns on pages 70-75.

Poodles Apron

Prim little poodles play well against the crisp green polka dots of this apron. Be stylish, wear your dots and look smart.
Patterns on page 47.

Pantaloons Apron

This whimsical apron reflects the care-free nature of the 1950's. Anything was fair game as you can see.
Patterns on page 50.

Handkerchiefs Apron

Red and white dots dance as you busily work in the kitchen. Cleverly folded pockets repeat the handkerchief patterns.
Patterns on page 46.

Black with Strawberries

Feisty strawberries on black entice sweet treats. Invite friends over for tea and crumpets and wow them with this adorable apron.
Patterns on page 48.

Aqua with Rick Rack

What a pretty apron. Nothing soothes the soul like soft colors and maybe a cup of tea.
Patterns on page 51.

Naughty Puppies Apron

These adorable puppies playing tug-of-war with Mother's clean laundry are sure to make you laugh.
Patterns on pages 44-45.

"dot.com" Aprons

Many aprons throughout history have exhibited polka dots in all sizes.

Note the "depression era" poodles on green apron panel that was available using all sizes of dots.

The 40's and 50's provided us with panels as in the green and black poodle apron. This era was known for red and white and 1950's kitchens sported many red and white aprons, like the bloomer style shown.

The "dot com" rage of the 21st Century also appreciates dots and relishes the nostalgic dots of the past.

The dot "coms" and dot "nets" keep the dots circulating! Patterns on pages 44-51.

This darling FLIP-FLOP Doll is three characters in one... the Wolf, Little Red Riding Hood and Grandma.

I see things I love and wish I had a little girl; then I realize that little girl could be me!

Happy Face Poem

Oh, I love my Dottie Doll
Because she's cute and round.
She sits upon my bed each night,
Not making any sound.
Her polka dots cheer up my room,
And make it very bright.
I hope you like my Dottie Doll,
And hug her, oh, so tight!

FLIP-FLOP Doll...

This clever little doll will inspire imagination in any child. She has one personality as a young girl and, with a flip of the wrist, can become Grandma or even the Big Bad Wolf! Patterns on pages 32-34.

Dresden Dottie

Red polka dots make a perfect frame for this happy pillow as it smiles at you from the center of an old-fashioned quilt block. Patterns on page 28.

Little Livia Huggy Doll

All dressed up, this little doll has long black braids and a cheery sunbonnet to match her bright red dress. Make her for that special little girl. Patterns on pages 35-40.

Dottie Pancake Doll

Dottie is both a huggable toy and a decorative pillow for some lucky child's room. Lay on her, play with her, hug her till you fall asleep. Patterns on pages 40-41.

Aunt Dottie Mae Doll

This doll recalls fond memories of women who lovingly cared for the families of others as well their own. Keep her dear to your heart. Patterns on pages 42-43.

Calico Cats Quilt

Are you a cat person? Well, if not, you soon will be when you make this cuddly quilt.

These cats are ever watchful and very well behaved; they stay in their place and never, never get under foot.

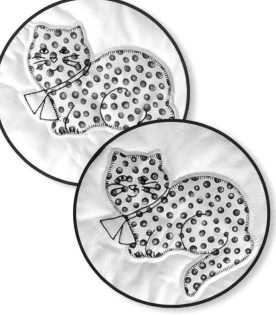

They're quiet and oh, so sweet. Snuggle up to one soon. It's the cat's meow!

Pattern on page 68.

Months of the Year

"Thirty days hath September..." We all know the rhyme.

Now there's another way to remember the months. Make this quilt and mark each month with an embroidered design befitting the season. Snowmen, flowers, ghosts and angels; this quilt has it all. You might even want to pick your favorite block and make a matching pillow. Let the fun begin.

Patterns on pages 80-89.

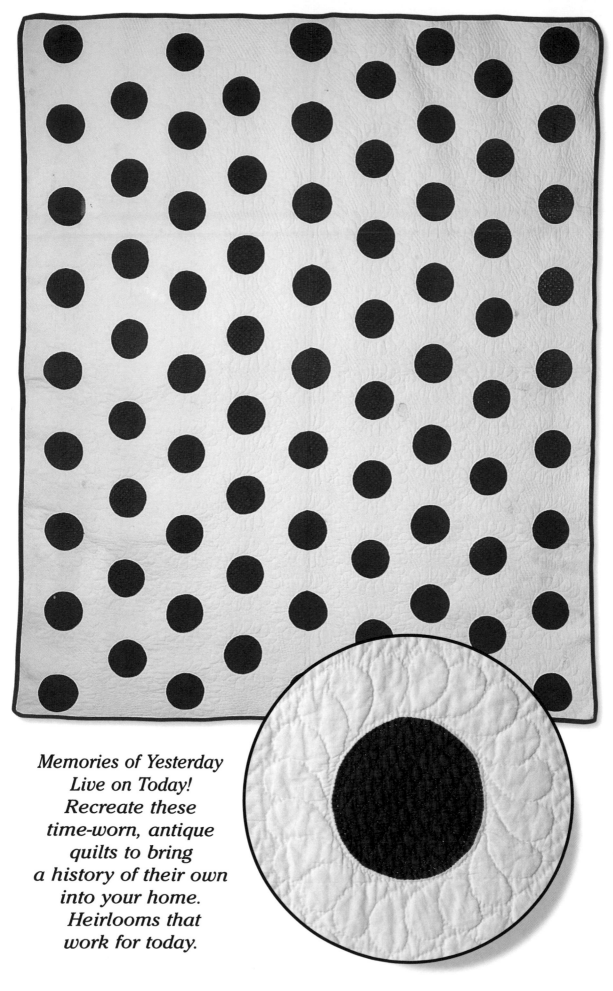

Big Dots Quilt

The maker of this unusual quilt with bold red dots should be commended for her creativity and excellent workmanship. The "Turkey Red" fabric is typical of Red and White quilts made in the U.S.A. from 1880 to 1910. This Red, however, was never produced in the United States. It was a difficult dyefast process discovered in Turkey, which lends the name. Turkey Red does not fade, but wears off in high relief areas like the circles in this quilt.

Red and White quilts from this era often have no borders. This was not so much a design consideration, but was due, primarily, to the high price of Turkey Red fabric.

This most unusual antique quilt by an unknown maker was purchased in Eureka, Missouri. This quilt is now part of the Red and White quilt collection of Ann Watkins Hazelwood where it is lovingly cared for.

Patterns on pages 30-31.

Memories of Yesterday Live on Today! Recreate these time-worn, antique quilts to bring a history of their own into your home. Heirlooms that work for today.

Polka Dots

The dot picked up the name "Polka Dot" from a popular Bohemian folk dance first introduced in Europe. The craze spread to the United States in 1845. Other consumer products picked up the name "Polka" as well, hoping to uplift retail sales. Such products were fishing lures, puddings and even hats.

Dots are of a happy and festive nature and are very easy to explain and visualize. Dots can be as small as "pin dots" to much larger or "oversized" as textile experts refer to them. Common sizes were called "coined size."

Dots have been consistently used by the fashion industry. No matter what color or trend develops, a "dot" can be added or even featured.

Starting about 1900, you'd more often than not find a dot used as the "resist" in an indigo or black mourning print. These two colors were popular and it was simple and inexpensive to use the dot design.

The 1920's and 1930's brought freshness and a much lighter look to garments, household furnishings and, of course, quilts. Pastel colors were well received, as all the catalogs and magazines touted. A 1926 Needlecraft magazine shows a lovely red and white child's dress for sale for $1.75. It is described as being made of Yomac, a novelty suiting of plain color interwoven with tiny white dots. Pockets and collar were of white pique. It was called the "Betsy" dress with matching bloomers, designed by Constance Wade.

A 1931 issue of Home Art Needlecraft magazine shows a Shirley Temple doll in a white dress with red polka dots. Shirley Temple, herself, shows the doll while wearing a matching dress. The doll was free if you sold six subscriptions to the magazine.

The 1930's promoted other fabrics, like a two-piece hand knit dress pattern that called for eleven one-ounce balls of a colored wool and one ball of white for the dot pattern scattered about the dress. This pattern could be ordered from Home Arts magazine for fifty cents.

Polka Star Quilt

"Starry, starry night" stars abound on this charming vintage quilt in red and white.

The longer you look, the more you see. Even the white dots on red become the dim stars of faraway galaxies.

Make this quilt and dream of worlds yet to be explored. Let your imagination soar!

Patterns on page 29.

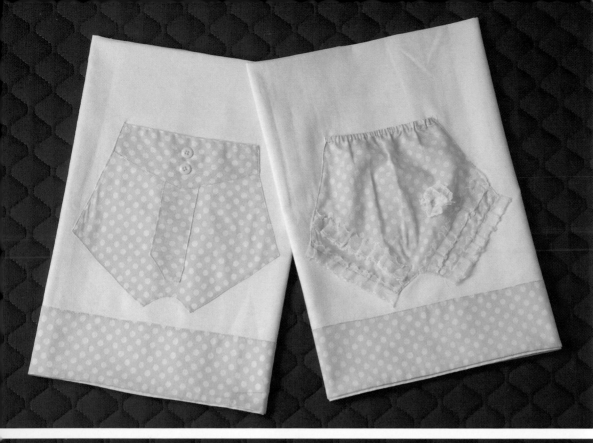

Shorts and Bloomers Pillowcases

What in the world? Shorts and bloomers adorn these aqua and white dot pillowcases.

What's next?

Around here, anything goes.

Patterns on pages 76-77.

Fruits Pillow

Brighten up a dark corner with this cheery pillow. Toss it on a breakfast room chair, make a pile of pillows for a day bed.

Anywhere you put them, these happy Red fruits and flower are bound to make you smile.

Patterns on pages 78-79.

Polka Dots
by Barbara Brackman

This is the story of a little girl named Dot, who loved dots.

Polka dots are a classic, easy to print and pleasant to view. Polka dots existed before they were called polka dots. The name comes from a Bohemian folk dance that was the rage in Paris in the 1840s, inspiring polka puddings and polka hats, as well as polka dots. The puddings are gone, but polka bands and polka dots remain.

Dot had polka dots on her party dress, on her underwear, and on her bathing suit.

Textile designers define a dot as a circular spot of color. The smallest dots are pin dots; the largest coin dots. I have a fragment of a quilt from about 1810 with a polka dot fabric in shades of brown; I could find a similar dot today.

Polka dots have had their fashion ups and downs. Dots were a craze in the 1930-1960 era, inspiring so many of the projects in this book. In the 1980s, Princess Diana wore polka dots to Fergie's wedding and an enormous rash of black and white spots broke out.

So she took a needle and thread and cloth, and she sewed and sewed,

And made a pocket big enough for Polka!

When I was growing up in the 1950s, my favorite comic book was Polka Dottie, who was a friend of Little Lulu's. Everything she owned, including her dog, had dots. I've tried to emulate her, but my friends and family keep imposing good taste. My dog has only one spot and my couch is plain green.

Barbara Brackman is a quilt and textile historian. She designs fabric for United Notions. Her most recent book is Prairie Flower: A Year on the Plains for the Kansas City Star.

Everybody liked Dot and her polka-dot pets so much that the judges gave them a special Grand Polka-Dot prize.

Clown Bean Bag

Photo on page 3

Clown Bean Bag Head Pattern
Cut 2   White or Flesh

FINISHED SIZE: 9¹/₂" tall

MATERIALS:

¹/₂ yard of 44" wide cotton Ecru polka dot fabric • 4" square of White knit fabric • 28" of 1" wide Ecru crocheted lace • 28" of Red ¹/₄" wide rickrack • 8" piece of Black knitting worsted yarn • Scraps of Black and Gold felt • ¹/₄" hole punch • 3 Red 1" pompons • Ecru sewing thread • Red and Tan embroidery flosses • Polyester stuffing • ¹/₂ cup of rice or beans

INSTRUCTIONS:

1. Use ¹/₄" seam allowances throughout.

2. Cut two 5¹/₂" x 9" piece of polka dot fabric for the body/legs. Cut the head, arms and hat patterns according to the patterns on page 21.

3. For the head, embroider the mouth with 3 strands of Red floss. Embroider the eyelashes with a single strand of Tan floss. Punch 2 Black felt ¹/₄" eye circles and a Gold felt nose circle. Sew eyes and nose in place. With right sides facing, sew a seam down the back of the head. Gather the bottom edge closed. Turn to right side. Stuff head firmly and gather the top closed. Lay head aside.

4. For the hat, with right sides facing, sew the straight sides together. Turn back seam allowance along the curved edge. Turn hat to right side, stuff firmly. Hand sew hat to head at a rakish angle. Fold the yarn in half and use Ecru thread to sew yarn to cover bottom edge of hat. Lay head aside.

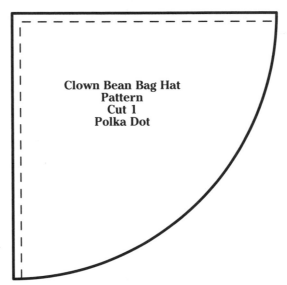

**Clown Bean Bag Hat
Pattern
Cut 1
Polka Dot**

**Clown Bean Bag Arm Pattern
Cut 2
Polka Dot**

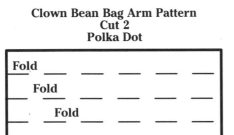

Fold

Fold

Fold

5. For the arms, fold each piece in half and fold the raw edges in to meet at the center. Sew down the center of each arm.

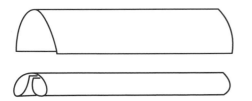

6. For the body/legs, locate the center of the fabric pieces and cut a 2¹/₄" slit from the bottom. With right sides facing, sew down the center of the body to the top of the slit. Pin the arms to the outer edges on the right side of one piece. Place arms 1¹/₂" below the top edge. With right sides facing, sew side seams. Gather the legs closed. Turn to the right side and pour ¹/₄ cup of rice or beans into each leg. Fold back the seam allowance and gather the top closed. Hand sew the bottom of the head to top of the gathers.

**Clown Bean Bag Body/Legs
Cut 2
Polka Dot**

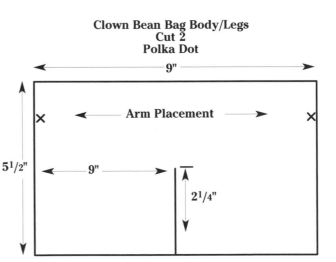

7. For the neck ruffle, cut a 12" and a 15" piece of each lace and rickrack. Hand sew the rickrack to the outer edge of each piece of lace. Sew the longer piece of lace along the center of the wrong side of the shorter piece. With right sides facing, sew the back center seam of the lace to form a circle. Gather the top edge of the lace assembly to fit around the neck. Stitch in place.

8. Glue or sew a pompon to the end of each arm and to the tip of the hat.

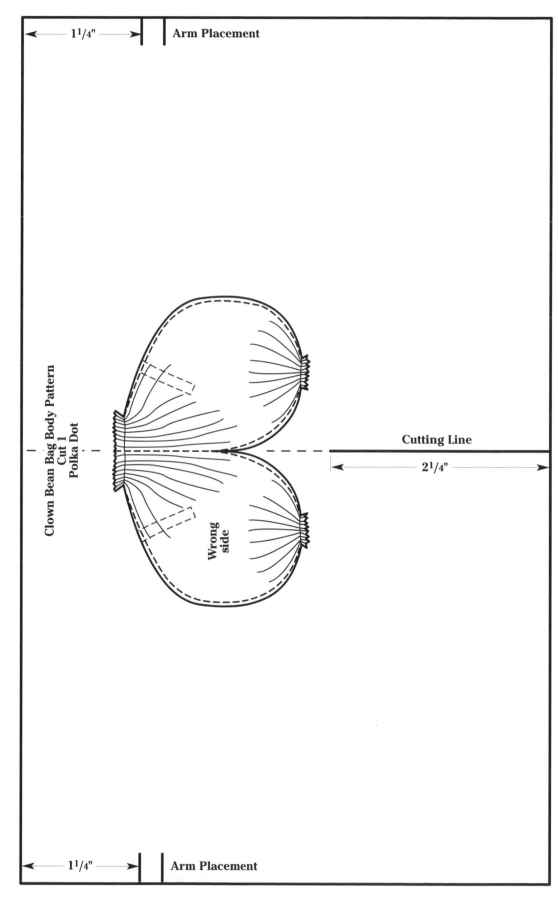

Arm Placement

← 1¹/₄" →

Clown Bean Bag Body Pattern
Cut 1
Polka Dot

Cutting Line

← 2¹/₄" →

Wrong
side

← 1¹/₄" →

Arm Placement

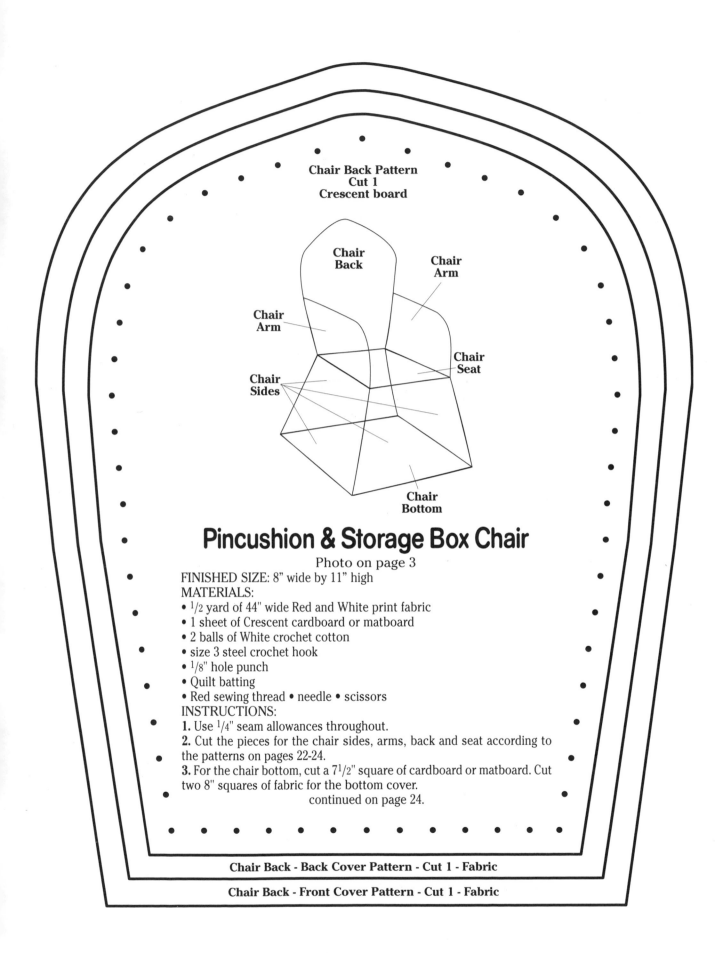

Chair Back Pattern
Cut 1
Crescent board

Chair
Back

Chair
Arm

Chair
Arm

Chair
Seat

Chair
Sides

Chair
Bottom

Pincushion & Storage Box Chair

Photo on page 3

FINISHED SIZE: 8" wide by 11" high

MATERIALS:
- $1/2$ yard of 44" wide Red and White print fabric
- 1 sheet of Crescent cardboard or matboard
- 2 balls of White crochet cotton
- size 3 steel crochet hook
- $1/8$" hole punch
- Quilt batting
- Red sewing thread • needle • scissors

INSTRUCTIONS:

1. Use $1/4$" seam allowances throughout.

2. Cut the pieces for the chair sides, arms, back and seat according to the patterns on pages 22-24.

3. For the chair bottom, cut a $7 1/2$" square of cardboard or matboard. Cut two 8" squares of fabric for the bottom cover.

continued on page 24.

Chair Back - Back Cover Pattern - Cut 1 - Fabric

Chair Back - Front Cover Pattern - Cut 1 - Fabric

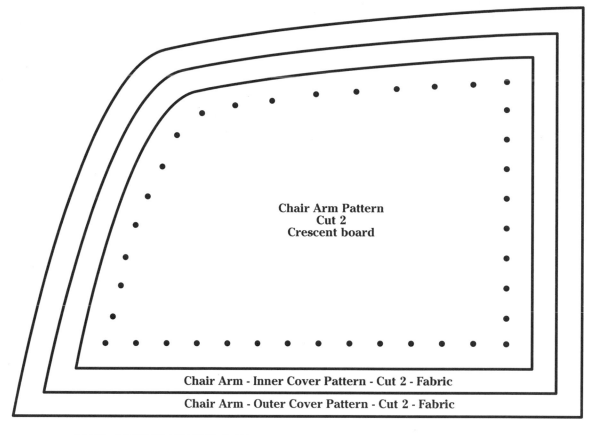

Chair Arm Pattern
Cut 2
Crescent board

Chair Arm - Inner Cover Pattern - Cut 2 - Fabric

Chair Arm - Outer Cover Pattern - Cut 2 - Fabric

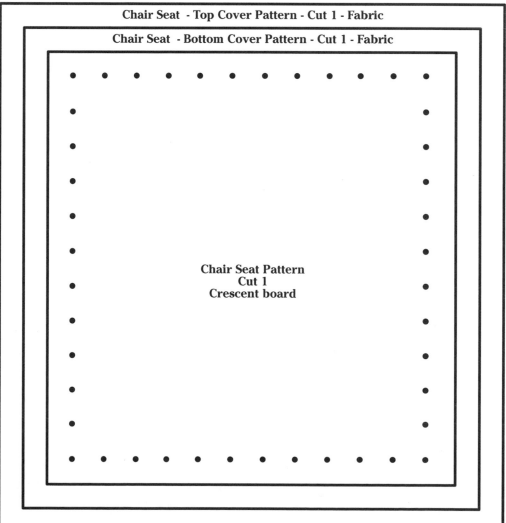

Chair Seat - Top Cover Pattern - Cut 1 - Fabric

Chair Seat - Bottom Cover Pattern - Cut 1 - Fabric

Chair Seat Pattern
Cut 1
Crescent board

Pincushion & Storage Box... continued from pages 22-23

4. Center chair bottom cardboard on wrong side of one piece of cover fabric. Fold edges of fabric over edges of board. Fold back the seam allowance on remaining piece of cover. Lay that piece right side facing on top of base. Hand sew folded edges to the piece of fabric covering the base around all edges. Repeat to cover each box side.

5. Center a cardboard arm on the wrong side of inner cover fabric. Fold edges of fabric over edges of base. Use 2 layers of quilt batting to pad center of crescent board before attaching outer cover fabric. Fold back the seam allowance on one outer cover fabric. Lay that piece on top of arm to cover quilt batting. Hand sew folded edges to the piece of fabric covering the arm around all edges. Repeat for other arm. The padded sides of the arms should be placed on the outside of the chair.

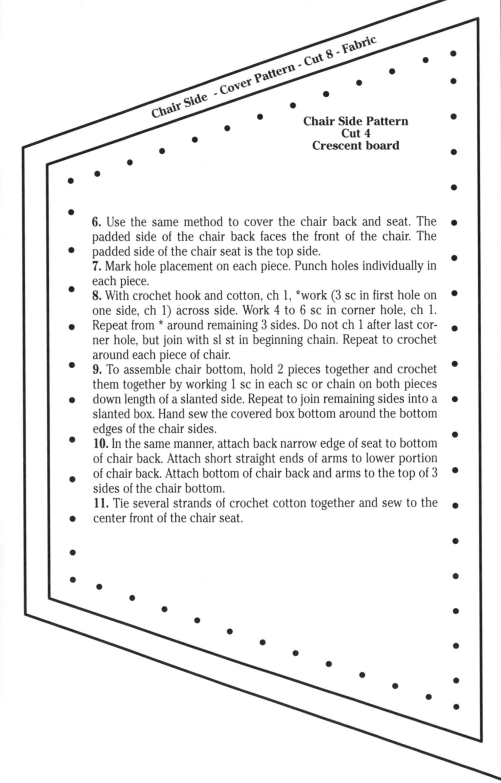

Chair Side - Cover Pattern - Cut 8 - Fabric

**Chair Side Pattern
Cut 4
Crescent board**

6. Use the same method to cover the chair back and seat. The padded side of the chair back faces the front of the chair. The padded side of the chair seat is the top side.

7. Mark hole placement on each piece. Punch holes individually in each piece.

8. With crochet hook and cotton, ch 1, *work (3 sc in first hole on one side, ch 1) across side. Work 4 to 6 sc in corner hole, ch 1. Repeat from * around remaining 3 sides. Do not ch 1 after last corner hole, but join with sl st in beginning chain. Repeat to crochet around each piece of chair.

9. To assemble chair bottom, hold 2 pieces together and crochet them together by working 1 sc in each sc or chain on both pieces down length of a slanted side. Repeat to join remaining sides into a slanted box. Hand sew the covered box bottom around the bottom edges of the chair sides.

10. In the same manner, attach back narrow edge of seat to bottom of chair back. Attach short straight ends of arms to lower portion of chair back. Attach bottom of chair back and arms to the top of 3 sides of the chair bottom.

11. Tie several strands of crochet cotton together and sew to the center front of the chair seat.

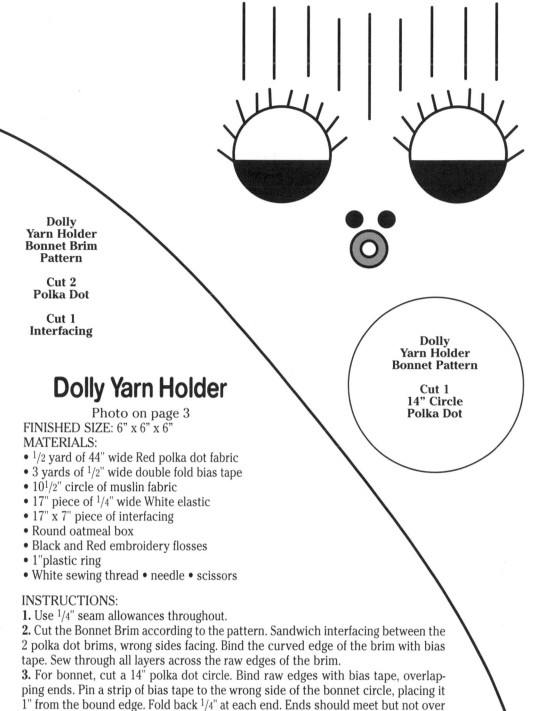

**Dolly
Yarn Holder
Bonnet Brim
Pattern**

**Cut 2
Polka Dot**

**Cut 1
Interfacing**

**Dolly
Yarn Holder
Bonnet Pattern**

**Cut 1
14" Circle
Polka Dot**

Dolly Yarn Holder

Photo on page 3

FINISHED SIZE: 6" x 6" x 6"

MATERIALS:

- $^1/_2$ yard of 44" wide Red polka dot fabric
- 3 yards of $^1/_2$" wide double fold bias tape
- $10^1/_2$" circle of muslin fabric
- 17" piece of $^1/_4$" wide White elastic
- 17" x 7" piece of interfacing
- Round oatmeal box
- Black and Red embroidery flosses
- 1"plastic ring
- White sewing thread • needle • scissors

INSTRUCTIONS:

1. Use $^1/_4$" seam allowances throughout.

2. Cut the Bonnet Brim according to the pattern. Sandwich interfacing between the 2 polka dot brims, wrong sides facing. Bind the curved edge of the brim with bias tape. Sew through all layers across the raw edges of the brim.

3. For bonnet, cut a 14" polka dot circle. Bind raw edges with bias tape, overlapping ends. Pin a strip of bias tape to the wrong side of the bonnet circle, placing it 1" from the bound edge. Fold back $^1/_4$" at each end. Ends should meet but not over lap. Sew both sides of bias tape in place to form a casing.

4. Transfer the face pattern to center of muslin circle. Embroider design. Carefully cut away fabric in the center of the mouth to form a hole for the yarn.

5. Cut oatmeal box to $3^1/_2$" tall. Discard top piece. Use a pencil to poke a hole in the bottom of the box $^1/_2$" from the edge. Place yarn in the box and pull end through hole. Pull yarn through mouth hole and place muslin circle across bottom of box. Fold edges of circle down onto sides of box and secure with a piece of string or a rubber band. Wrap the Bonnet Brim around the box, aligning the raw edges of the brim with the bottom of the box and overlapping ends. Secure ends. Make certain the brim is centered above the face design.

6. Thread elastic through the casing on the Bonnet. Set covered box inside the Bonnet, open end down. Pull the elastic to gather the bonnet to fit snugly around box. Overlap the ends of elastic 1" and sew together at the center back of Bonnet. Pull gathers even. For hanger, sew a plastic ring to Bonnet above center of brim.

Place on fold

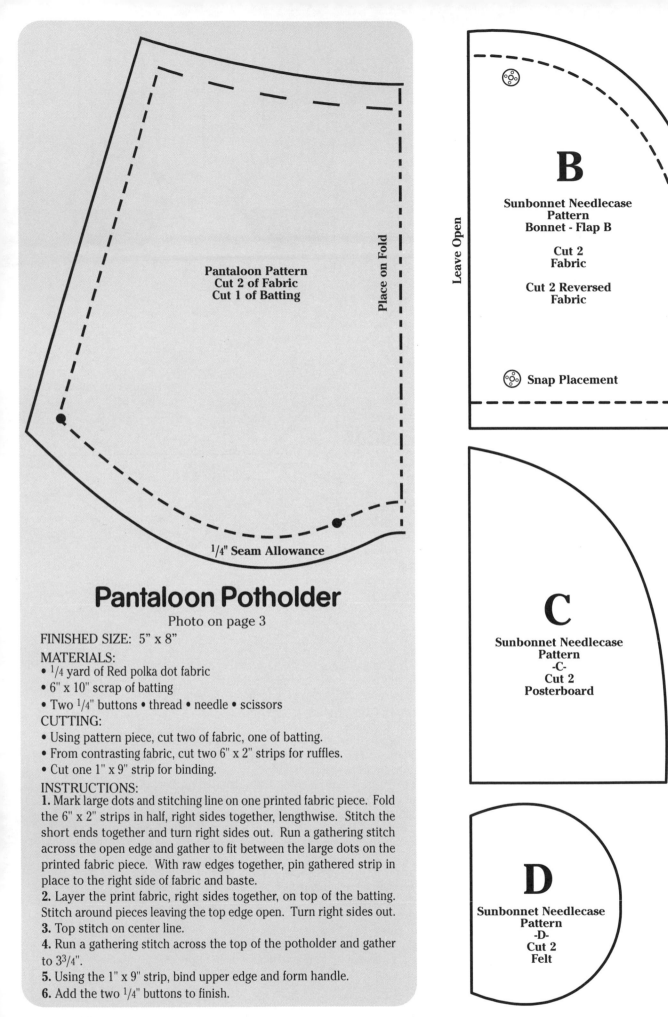

**Pantaloon Pattern
Cut 2 of Fabric
Cut 1 of Batting**

Place on Fold

1/4" Seam Allowance

Leave Open

B

**Sunbonnet Needlecase
Pattern
Bonnet - Flap B**

**Cut 2
Fabric**

**Cut 2 Reversed
Fabric**

Snap Placement

C

**Sunbonnet Needlecase
Pattern
-C-
Cut 2
Posterboard**

D

**Sunbonnet Needlecase
Pattern
-D-
Cut 2
Felt**

Pantaloon Potholder

Photo on page 3

FINISHED SIZE: 5" x 8"

MATERIALS:
- 1/4 yard of Red polka dot fabric
- 6" x 10" scrap of batting
- Two 1/4" buttons • thread • needle • scissors

CUTTING:
- Using pattern piece, cut two of fabric, one of batting.
- From contrasting fabric, cut two 6" x 2" strips for ruffles.
- Cut one 1" x 9" strip for binding.

INSTRUCTIONS:
1. Mark large dots and stitching line on one printed fabric piece. Fold the 6" x 2" strips in half, right sides together, lengthwise. Stitch the short ends together and turn right sides out. Run a gathering stitch across the open edge and gather to fit between the large dots on the printed fabric piece. With raw edges together, pin gathered strip in place to the right side of fabric and baste.
2. Layer the print fabric, right sides together, on top of the batting. Stitch around pieces leaving the top edge open. Turn right sides out.
3. Top stitch on center line.
4. Run a gathering stitch across the top of the potholder and gather to 3 3/4".
5. Using the 1" x 9" strip, bind upper edge and form handle.
6. Add the two 1/4" buttons to finish.

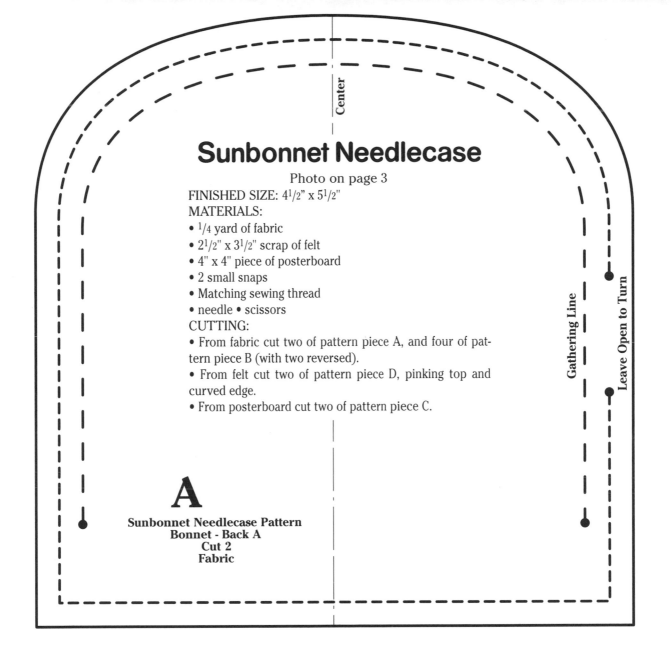

Sunbonnet Needlecase

Photo on page 3

FINISHED SIZE: 4¹/2" x 5¹/2"

MATERIALS:
- ¹/4 yard of fabric
- 2¹/2" x 3¹/2" scrap of felt
- 4" x 4" piece of posterboard
- 2 small snaps
- Matching sewing thread
- needle • scissors

CUTTING:
- From fabric cut two of pattern piece A, and four of pattern piece B (with two reversed).
- From felt cut two of pattern piece D, pinking top and curved edge.
- From posterboard cut two of pattern piece C.

Center

Gathering Line

Leave Open to Turn

A
Sunbonnet Needlecase Pattern
Bonnet - Back A
Cut 2
Fabric

INSTRUCTIONS:
1. With right sides together, stitch around bonnet piece A using a ¹/4" seam and leaving a small opening for turning.
2. Clip curves as needed and turn right sides out. Stitch closed the opening in seam by hand.
3. Run a gathering stitch around the bonnet as marked.
4. Fold the bonnet in half and mark the center top. Set aside.
5. With right sides together, sew around the top and curved edge of pattern piece B, leaving the straight edge open.
6. Clip curves and trim point. Turn right sides out and insert the posterboard piece C. Turn in edges and handstitch together. Repeat with the remaining bonnet flap.

ASSEMBLY:
7. Sew bonnet flap and felt to edge of bonnet as shown. Repeat for other side.
8. Run gathering stitch along bottom of bonnet; pull tight. Sew snaps.

Patterns continue on page 26

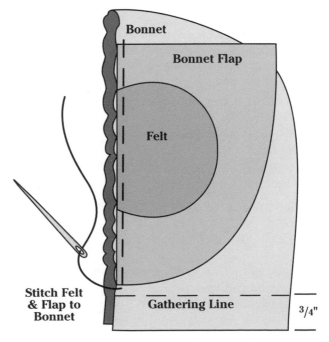

Bonnet

Bonnet Flap

Felt

Stitch Felt & Flap to Bonnet

Gathering Line

3/4"

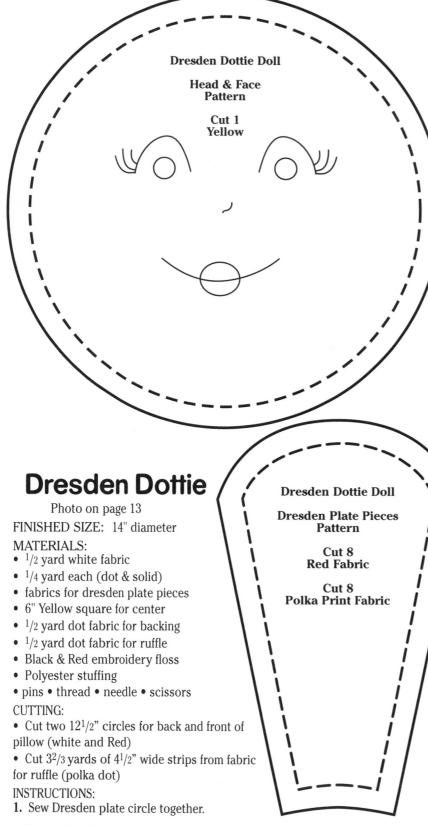

Dresden Dottie Doll

Head & Face
Pattern

Cut 1
Yellow

Dresden Dottie Doll

Dresden Plate Pieces
Pattern

Cut 8
Red Fabric

Cut 8
Polka Print Fabric

Flower Garden Potholder Pattern

Flower Garden
Potholder
Pattern

Cut 19
Template
Shapes

Flower Garden Potholder

Photo on page 3

FINISHED SIZE: 8^1/$_2$" diameter

TIP: Use ^{1}/$_4$" seam allowances.

MATERIALS:
• 3" square of Yellow fabric for center
• 6" x 9" Red fabric for middle row
• 9" x 12" Red polka dot fabric for outside row
• Two 10" squares of muslin for front & back
• 1 yard of ^{1}/$_2$" single fold bias binding
• 10" square of quilt batting
• pins • thread • needle • scissors

CUTTING:
• Cut 1 Yellow hexagon
• Cut 6 Red hexagons
• Cut 12 Polka Dot hexagons

INSTRUCTIONS:
1. Place cardstock or paper pattern piece on wrong side of fabric and pin in place (iron freezer paper in place).
2. Fold the ^{1}/$_4$" seam allowance over template and baste into position.
3. Place right sides together, sew fabric pieces together with small whip stitches.
4. When all pieces are sewn together, press lightly. Template pieces are still in place.
5. Center the joined hexagon pieces on the 9" circle of fabric and appliqué.
6. Turn piece over and trim background fabric to within ^{1}/$_4$" from appliqué stitching, then remove the trimmed excess.
7. Pull out the basting threads and remove pattern papers. They can be used again.
8. Layer the top piece, batting and the back and base across with large stitches.
9. Hand quilt around inside of the center and inside edge to the next two rows. Hand quilt the outside design.
10. Sew bias tape to the circle and make a loop to hang it.

Dresden Dottie

Photo on page 13

FINISHED SIZE: 14" diameter

MATERIALS:
• ^{1}/$_2$ yard white fabric
• ^{1}/$_4$ yard each (dot & solid)
• fabrics for dresden plate pieces
• 6" Yellow square for center
• ^{1}/$_2$ yard dot fabric for backing
• ^{1}/$_2$ yard dot fabric for ruffle
• Black & Red embroidery floss
• Polyester stuffing
• pins • thread • needle • scissors

CUTTING:
• Cut two 12^1/$_2$" circles for back and front of pillow (white and Red)
• Cut 3^2/$_3$ yards of 4^1/$_2$" wide strips from fabric for ruffle (polka dot)

INSTRUCTIONS:
1. Sew Dresden plate circle together.
2. Center Dresden plate on background circle and appliqué by hand or machine.
3. Embroider Dottie face, using a running or backstitch for lines and satin stitch for mouth and dots in eyes. Appliqué center circle.
4. Piece together the 4^1/$_2$" strips, fold in half lengthwise and press. Gather to make a generous ruffle. Pin in place around one side of pillow. Pin other half of pillow, with right sides together, ruffle facing the inside. Sew a ^{1}/$_4$" seam around pillow, leaving an opening about 4" long so you can turn the pillow right side out.
5. Turn right side out, stuff firmly and hand close the opening.
"Dresden Dottie" will be a smiling face waiting for you. Enjoy!

The Polka Star Quilt
Traditional Ohio Star Pattern
Photo on page 17

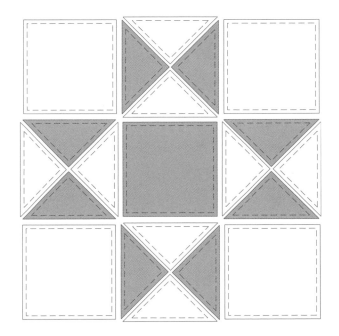

FINISHED SIZE: 37" x 37"

MATERIALS:

- 1 yard muslin fabric
- 1 1/2 yard Red dot fabric
- 1 1/4 yard of backing fabric
- Quilt batting
- 5 yards of 3/8" double fold bias binding
- 36 assorted buttons - 7/16" to 7/8"
- pins • thread • needle • scissors

TIP: These vintage 1930's blocks are directly connected in a direct setting.

CUTTING:

Cut the following to create one block:

- 8 triangles in Red dot fabric
- 8 triangles in muslin
- Four 2 1/2" squares of muslin
- One 2 1/2" square of Red dot fabric

TIP: Use 1/8" seams throughout (on this quilt only, all other projects use 1/4" seams).

**Polka Star
Quilt Pattern**

Square

1/8" Seam Allowance

**Polka Star
Quilt Pattern**

Triangle

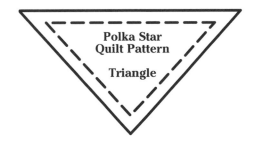

INSTRUCTIONS:

1. Use a 1/8" seam for piecing, marking the seam allowances, if necessary.

2. Assemble each block as shown.

3. Sew together in rows of seven blocks to create a square quilt for the wall or a crib quilt for a baby.

4. Layer top, batting, backing. Add binding.

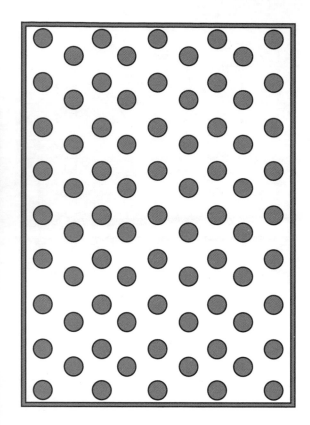

Big Dots Quilt

Photo on page 16

FINISHED SIZE: 68$\frac{1}{2}$" x 78"

TIP: Use $\frac{1}{4}$" seam allowances.

MATERIALS:

- 5 yards of White fabric for top
  or TIP: Use 2$\frac{1}{2}$ yards of 72" wide fabric
  (White cotton fabric 72" wide is often
  available in the quilt department)
- 5 yards of solid fabric for bottom
- 1$\frac{1}{2}$ yards of Red fabric for circles
- 9 yards of $\frac{1}{2}$" double fold Red bias binding
- Quilt batting
- pins • thread • needle • scissors

CUTTING:

- Cut 77 circles 5" in diameter from Red fabric
- Cut two 2$\frac{1}{2}$ yard panels of background fabric
- Cut two 2$\frac{1}{2}$ yard panels of backing fabric
- Sew lengths of bias tape together to make a continuous 9 yard strip

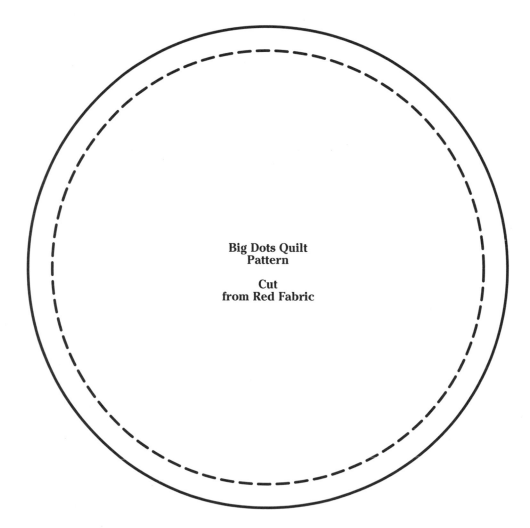

**Big Dots Quilt
Pattern**

**Cut
from Red Fabric**

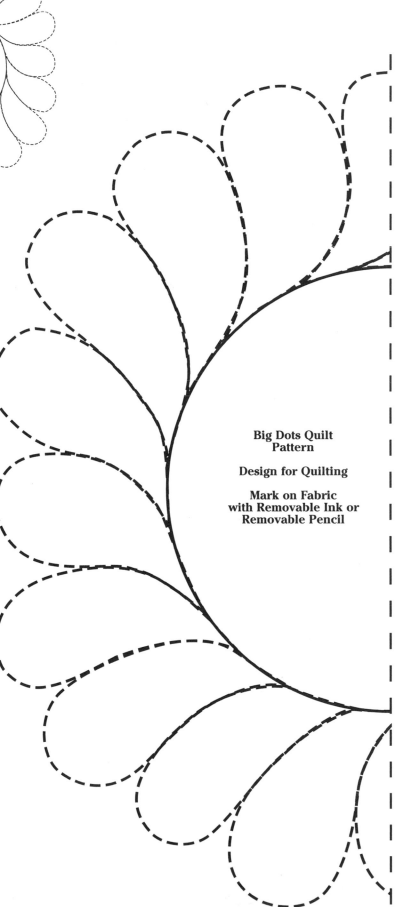

Design for Quilting

INSTRUCTIONS:

1. Use one length of 72" wide fabric OR Sew the 2 background 36-44" wide panels together on one long side.

2. Mark placement of all dots and quilting lines on backing fabric. Applique dots in place.

3. Sandwich layers as follows: top (facing out), batting, then backing (facing out). Pin or baste in place. Quilt along all marked lines. The antique sample shows $1/2$" cross hatching in circles, feathering around the circles and $1/2$" apart diagonal lines in all other background areas.

4. Bind the edges with binding. With right sides facing, sew strip ends together. Press seams open. Sew strips to back of quilt, fold back $1/4$" along raw edge. Fold over, whip stitch in place.

Big Dots Quilt Pattern

Design for Quilting

Mark on Fabric with Removable Ink or Removable Pencil

Flip Flop Doll

Photo on page 12

FINISHED SIZE: 14" tall

MATERIALS:

- 1 yard of 44" wide Red and White polka dot fabric
- 1 yard of 44" wide White and Black polka dot fabric
- $1/2$ yard of muslin fabric
- $1/2$ yard of White fabric • scrap of Red fabric
- 20" of $1/4$" Red satin ribbon
- 1 yard of $1/4$" Ecru lace trim
- 19" of $1/2$" White double-fold bias binding
- Brown, Red, Blue, Gray and Pink fabric paint pens
- Scrap of Yellow rug yarn
- Scrap of Gray rug yarn
- Polyester stuffing
- pins • thread • needle • scissors

INSTRUCTIONS:

1. Use $1/4$" seam allowances throughout.

2. Cut the body, bodice, kerchief, dickie and apron according to the patterns on pages 32 - 35.

3. Transfer Red Riding Hood and Granny face patterns to either end of the body pieces. Paint faces, allow to dry.

4. With right sides facing, sew body pieces together. Leave an opening on one side. Turn to right side, stuff doll firmly. Fold back seam allowance and hand sew opening closed. Stitch dickies in place.

5. With right sides facing, sew underarm and side seam on bodice pieces. Fold back seam allowance along center front of each piece, press. Fold back $1/8$" twice along sleeve ends, topstitch. For dickies, cut a $3^1/2$" x 6" piece of Red fabric for Girl and a $3^1/2$" x 6" piece of White fabric for Granny. Fold each piece in half to measure $3^1/2$" x 3". Place folded edge across neck and hand sew all edges to front of doll. Place one White/Black bodice on Granny end. Hand stitch bodice edges to doll. Place other bodice on doll, overlapping front edges. Sew in place by hand. Repeat for Red/White pieces on girl.

6. For skirts, cut a 46" x 9" piece of Red/White fabric for Girl, cut a 46" x 9" piece of White/Black fabric for Granny. With right sides facing, sew skirts together along one long edge. Press seam open. With right sides facing, sew back center seam across both skirts, forming a tube. Turn to right side, align raw edges and press hem edge. Gather each remaining long raw edge to measure 7". Pull gathers even. For waistbands, cut a matching $7^1/2$" x $1^1/2$" piece of each fabric. Sew short ends, right sides together. Repeat for other skirt fabric. With right sides together, pin each waistband to each skirt, adjusting gathers. Sew waistband and gathered edge of skirt together (see illustration). Fold back seam allowance along to raw edges of waistband and hand sew in place to cover bottom raw edges of each bodice.

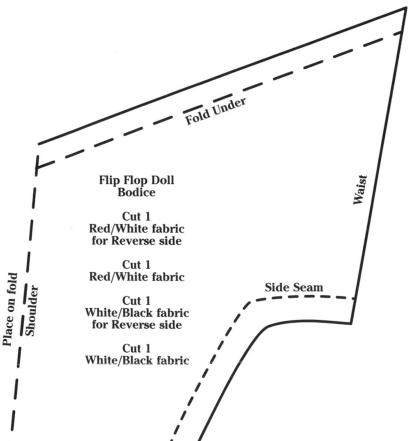

**Flip Flop Doll
Kerchief Pattern**

**Cut 1
Red/White
Fabric**

Fold Under

Waist

**Flip Flop Doll
Bodice**

**Cut 1
Red/White fabric
for Reverse side**

**Cut 1
Red/White fabric**

**Cut 1
White/Black fabric
for Reverse side**

**Cut 1
White/Black fabric**

Place on fold

Shoulder

Side Seam

Sleeve Edge

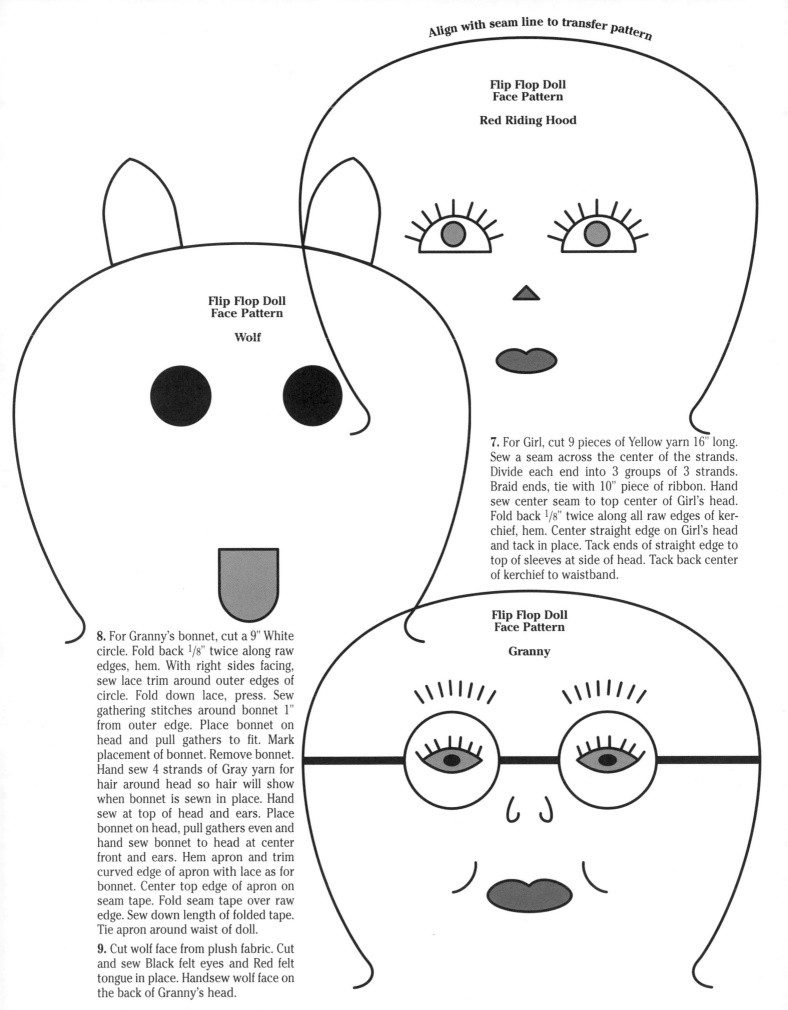

**Flip Flop Doll
Face Pattern**

Red Riding Hood

**Flip Flop Doll
Face Pattern**

Wolf

7. For Girl, cut 9 pieces of Yellow yarn 16" long. Sew a seam across the center of the strands. Divide each end into 3 groups of 3 strands. Braid ends, tie with 10" piece of ribbon. Hand sew center seam to top center of Girl's head. Fold back 1/8" twice along all raw edges of kerchief, hem. Center straight edge on Girl's head and tack in place. Tack ends of straight edge to top of sleeves at side of head. Tack back center of kerchief to waistband.

**Flip Flop Doll
Face Pattern**

Granny

8. For Granny's bonnet, cut a 9" White circle. Fold back 1/8" twice along raw edges, hem. With right sides facing, sew lace trim around outer edges of circle. Fold down lace, press. Sew gathering stitches around bonnet 1" from outer edge. Place bonnet on head and pull gathers to fit. Mark placement of bonnet. Remove bonnet. Hand sew 4 strands of Gray yarn for hair around head so hair will show when bonnet is sewn in place. Hand sew at top of head and ears. Place bonnet on head, pull gathers even and hand sew bonnet to head at center front and ears. Hem apron and trim curved edge of apron with lace as for bonnet. Center top edge of apron on seam tape. Fold seam tape over raw edge. Sew down length of folded tape. Tie apron around waist of doll.

9. Cut wolf face from plush fabric. Cut and sew Black felt eyes and Red felt tongue in place. Handsew wolf face on the back of Granny's head.

Patterns continued on page 34

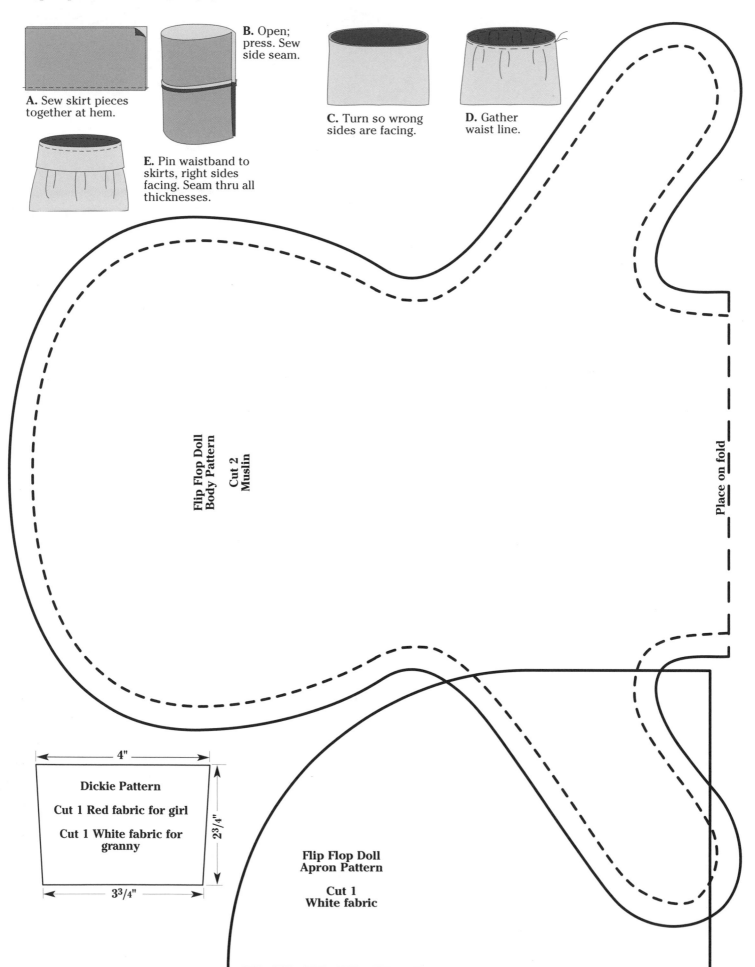

A. Sew skirt pieces together at hem.

B. Open; press. Sew side seam.

C. Turn so wrong sides are facing.

D. Gather waist line.

E. Pin waistband to skirts, right sides facing. Seam thru all thicknesses.

Flip Flop Doll
Body Pattern

**Cut 2
Muslin**

Place on fold

4"

Dickie Pattern

Cut 1 Red fabric for girl

Cut 1 White fabric for granny

2³/4"

3³/4"

**Flip Flop Doll
Apron Pattern**

**Cut 1
White fabric**

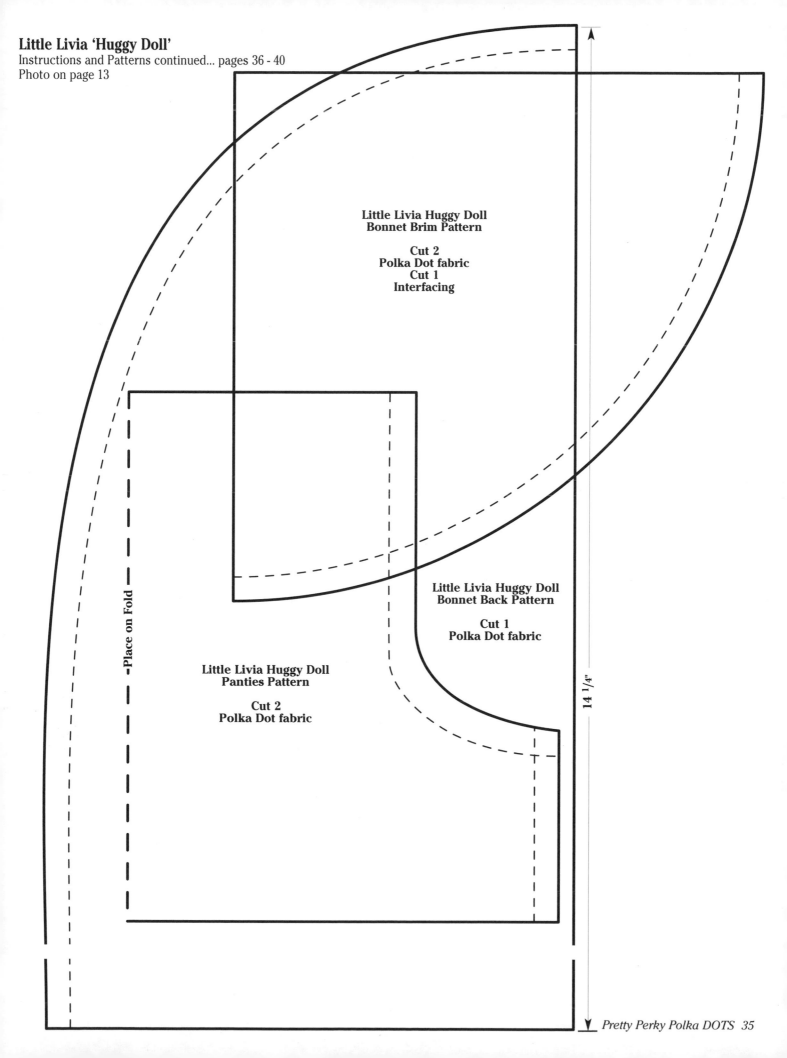

Little Livia 'Huggy Doll'
Instructions and Patterns continued... pages 36 - 40
Photo on page 13

Little Livia Huggy Doll
Bonnet Brim Pattern

Cut 2
Polka Dot fabric
Cut 1
Interfacing

Little Livia Huggy Doll
Bonnet Back Pattern

Cut 1
Polka Dot fabric

-Place on Fold

Little Livia Huggy Doll
Panties Pattern

Cut 2
Polka Dot fabric

14 ¼"

Little Livia 'Huggy Doll'

Photo on page 13

FINISHED SIZE: 16" tall

MATERIALS:

- $1/2$ yard of 44" wide Brown fabric
- $1/2$ yard of 44" wide Red and White polka dot fabric
- 43" x 7" piece of Red netting
- 3 yards of $1/2$" White rick rack • 40" of $1/4$" Red satin ribbon
- 15" of $1/2$" Red Satin ribbon
- Square of Red felt
- 2 White pearl $1/2$" shank buttons
- 12" of $1/4$" wide elastic
- Scrap of Black knitting worsted yarn
- Red, Black and White embroidery flosses
- Brown, Red and White sewing threads
- Pinking shears
- Polyester stuffing
- 5" x 10" piece interfacing
- pins • thread • needle • scissors

INSTRUCTIONS:

1. Use $1/4$" seam allowances throughout.

2. Cut the body, gussets, arm, leg, panties, dress, bonnet and shoes according to the patterns on pages 36 -40.

3. With right sides facing, sew the body gussets together across the short straight edges.

4. Sew the darts on each of the side body pieces. With right sides facing, sew body pieces to either side of the gusset strip, aligning the seam in the gusset with the line at the top of the side body. Leave an opening at the bottom. Clip curves as necessary. Turn to right side. Transfer facial features to doll and embroider. Stuff doll firmly. Fold back seam allowance and hand sew opening closed. Lay body aside.

5. With right sides facing, sew 2 arm pieces together, leaving an opening along one side. Turn to right side, stuff arm firmly. Fold back seam allowance and hand sew opening closed. Repeat with other arm. Use a long needle and Brown thread to sew arms to either side of the body at points indicated on patterns. Sew several times through arms and body to secure. Secure thread end.

6. For legs, sew and stuff as for arms, above. Sew to body in the same manner. Lay doll aside.

7. With right sides facing, sew crotch seam on panties. Turn back $1/8$" twice on one leg. Hold $9^{1}/_{2}$" of rickrack on wrong side and topstitch. Repeat on other leg. Sew leg seam. Fold back $1/8$" along top edge then fold back $3/8$" to form casing. Sew casing in place, leaving a 2" opening. Insert elastic into casing. Place panties on doll, adjust elastic and overlap ends. Sew across ends. Sew open-ing closed.

8. For petticoat, fold netting in half lengthwise. Gather folded edge to 9". Sew $1/2$" ribbon across gathers, centering netting on ribbon. Place petticoat on doll, tie ribbon ends at back.

9. Sew shoulder seam of bodice pieces, right sides facing. Begin 1" from seam line of one sleeve to gather center of sleeve to fit armhole. Sew sleeve in place. Sew underarm seam on sleeve and bodice, right sides facing and aligning raw edges of pieces. Gather outer edge of sleeve. With right sides facing, sew across ends of an armband to form a circle. Fold armband in half along center line, fold back $1/8$" along each raw edge. Pin to sleeve, adjust gathers. Hand sew armband to cover raw edge of sleeve. Repeat for other sleeve.

10. For skirt, cut a 36" x $6^{3}/_{4}$" piece of Red/White fabric. Fold back $1/8$" twice along hem edge. Hold 36" of rickrack on wrong side and topstitch. Gather top edge of skirt to fit lower edge of bodice from seam line to seam line. Pull gathers even and with right sides facing, sew skirt to bodice. With right sides facing, sew back center seam of skirt from hem edge, stopping $1^{1}/_{4}$" below top of skirt. Fold back $1/8$" along both sides of back open-ing of bodice, topstitch. Use White thread to sew a row of rick-rack around waist. Fold back $1/8$" once along raw neck edge. Use zigzag stitch to sew a piece of rick rack neck edge. Sew a snap set to the back bodice opening at waist. Sew other snap set at neckline. Place dress on doll.

11. For hair, cut 30 pieces of yarn 28" long. Lay the yarn pieces side by side so they measure about $1^{1}/_{2}$" across and stitch down the center of the pieces. Pull the strands together 5" down from one side of center. Divide ends into 3 groups of 10 strands and braid ends together. Tie a $7^{1}/_{2}$" piece of $1/4$" ribbon around bottom of braid. Tack top of braid to side of head. Repeat on other end. Hand sew center of braid to top center of head. For back of hair, cut 24 pieces of yarn 16" long. Lay pieces side by side and sew center seam. Hand sew center to head behind braids.

12. For bonnet, sew interfacing to wrong side of one bonnet brim around curved edge. Trim interfacing close to seam. Baste or pin a strip of rickrack around the curved edge along seam line. Fold back seam allowance along straight edge of each bon-net brim piece. With right sides facing, sew around curved edge, catching rickrack in seam. Turn to right side. Fold back $1/8$" twice along bottom edge of bonnet back, gather edge to measure 5". Insert straight raw edge of bonnet back into bonnet brim between pieces, topstitch. Cut two 12" pieces of $1/2$" rib-bon. Fold back $1/2$" at one end and sew to lower edge of bonnet just behind brim. Repeat with another piece of ribbon on other side. Place bonnet on doll and tie ribbon ends in a bow.

Instructions and Patterns continued... pages 36 - 40.

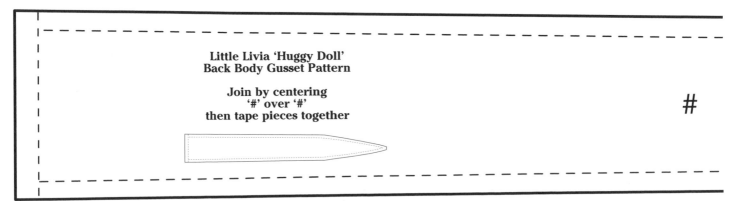

Little Livia 'Huggy Doll'
Back Body Gusset Pattern

Join by centering
'#' over '#'
then tape pieces together

\#

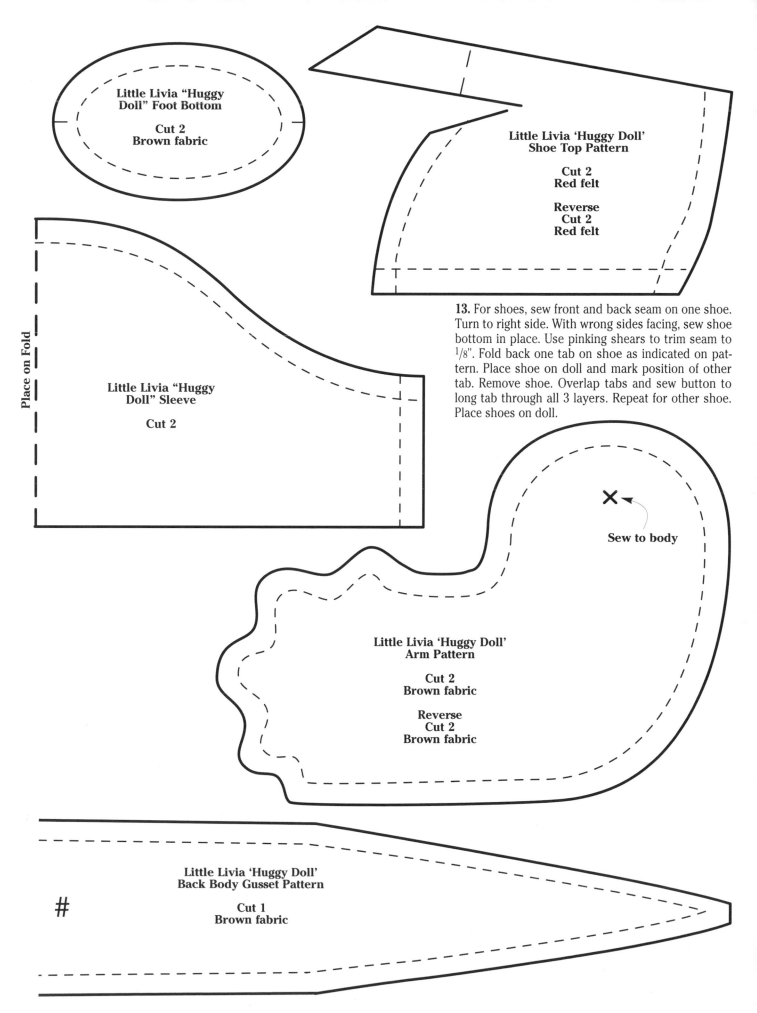

Little Livia "Huggy Doll" Foot Bottom

Cut 2
Brown fabric

Little Livia 'Huggy Doll' Shoe Top Pattern

Cut 2
Red felt

Reverse
Cut 2
Red felt

Place on Fold

Little Livia "Huggy Doll" Sleeve

Cut 2

13. For shoes, sew front and back seam on one shoe. Turn to right side. With wrong sides facing, sew shoe bottom in place. Use pinking shears to trim seam to $1/8$". Fold back one tab on shoe as indicated on pattern. Place shoe on doll and mark position of other tab. Remove shoe. Overlap tabs and sew button to long tab through all 3 layers. Repeat for other shoe. Place shoes on doll.

✕← Sew to body

Little Livia 'Huggy Doll' Arm Pattern

Cut 2
Brown fabric

Reverse
Cut 2
Brown fabric

#

Little Livia 'Huggy Doll' Back Body Gusset Pattern

Cut 1
Brown fabric

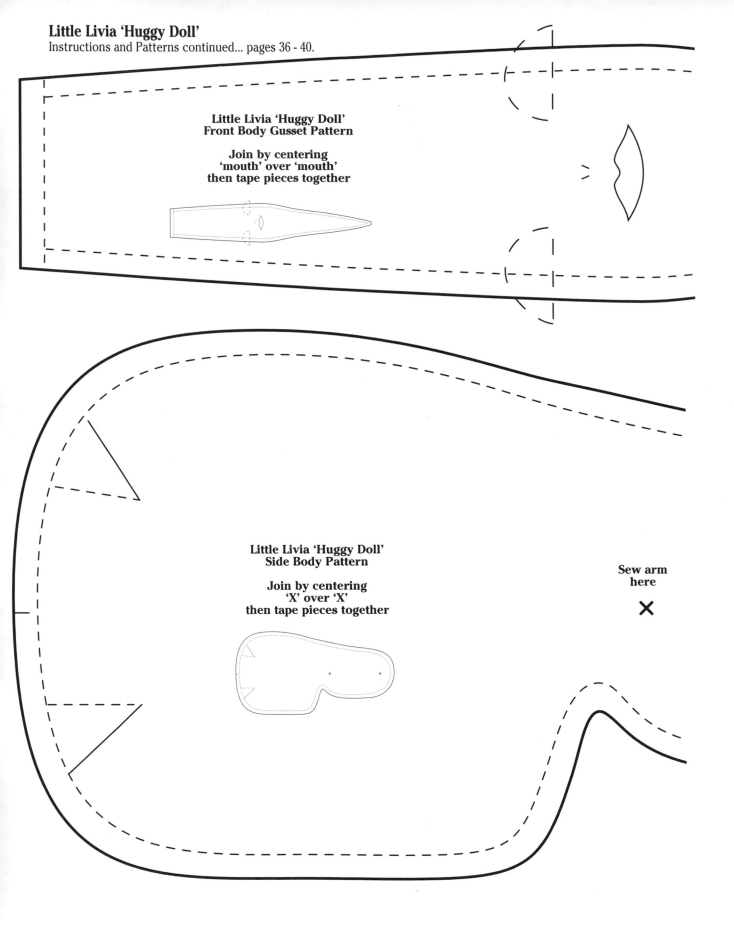

Little Livia 'Huggy Doll'
Front Body Gusset Pattern

**Join by centering
'mouth' over 'mouth'
then tape pieces together**

Little Livia 'Huggy Doll'
Side Body Pattern

**Join by centering
'X' over 'X'
then tape pieces together**

**Sew arm
here**

X

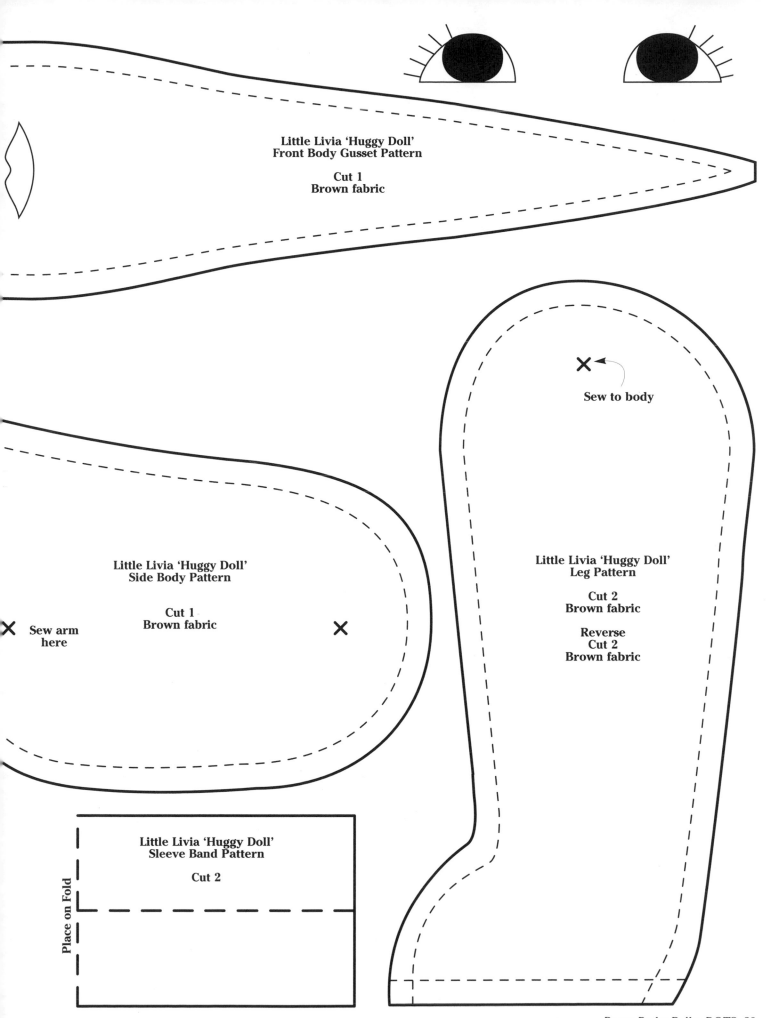

Little Livia 'Huggy Doll'
Front Body Gusset Pattern

Cut 1
Brown fabric

Sew to body

Little Livia 'Huggy Doll'
Side Body Pattern

Cut 1
Brown fabric

Sew arm
here

Little Livia 'Huggy Doll'
Leg Pattern

Cut 2
Brown fabric

Reverse
Cut 2
Brown fabric

Little Livia 'Huggy Doll'
Sleeve Band Pattern

Cut 2

Place on Fold

Little Livia 'Huggy Doll'
Instructions and Patterns
continued... pages 36 - 40.

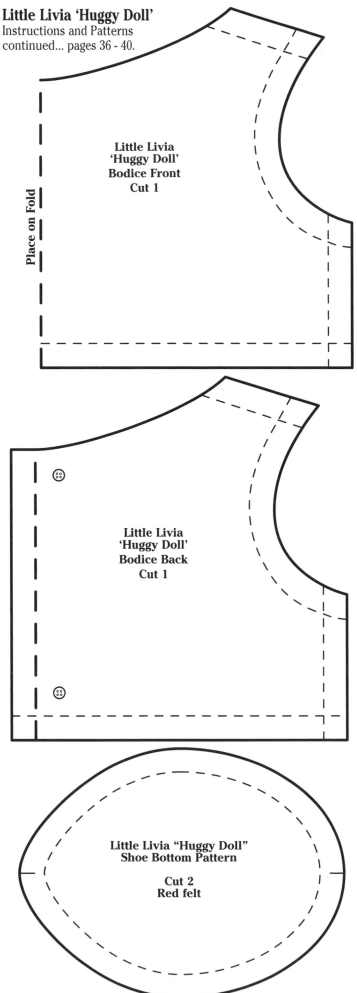

Place on Fold

Little Livia
'Huggy Doll'
Bodice Front
Cut 1

Little Livia
'Huggy Doll'
Bodice Back
Cut 1

Little Livia "Huggy Doll"
Shoe Bottom Pattern

**Cut 2
Red felt**

Dottie Pancake Doll
Photo on page 13

FINISHED SIZE: $10^1/2$" x 15"

MATERIALS:
- $1/2$ yard of Red dot fabric
- $1/8$ yard of Black fabric
- $1/4$ yard of Yellow fabric
- $1/4$ yard of muslin fabric
- 8" length of $1/4$" wide Black satin ribbon
- Red and White polka dot button
- Red and Black embroidery floss
- Polyester stuffing
- pins • thread • needle • scissors

TIPS: Trace pattern shape and facial features onto muslin and embroider face before cutting.

CUTTING:
- Cut embroidered face piece from muslin.
- Cut 1 front hair from Yellow fabric.
- Cut 1 back hair from Yellow fabric.
- Cut two 12" circles from Red dot fabric.
- Cut 2 hands from muslin.
- Cut 2 shoes from black fabric.

INSTRUCTIONS:

1. Before cutting, trace face pattern and features onto muslin. Embroider face with red and black floss.

2. Stitch outline of hair onto face with natural colored thread. Baste or pin hair pattern piece to face. With natural colored thread, sew in place with a blanket stitch. Adding $1/4$" seam allowance, cut face circle out.

3. With wrong sides together, sew head front to head back, leaving opening at neck edge to insert batting. Turn right side out. Insert batting. Hand stitch opening closed.

4. Stitch outline of hands, as marked on pattern piece, onto right side of one body circle with natural colored thread, making sure dots are aligned the way you prefer and one hand is reversed, thumbs toward face. Sew in place with a blanket stitch.

5. Stitch outline of shoes with black thread, as marked on pattern piece, onto right side of circle, remembering to reverse one. Sew in place using a blanket stitch.

6. With wrong sides facing, pin body back to front, aligning dots the same direction as on front. Pin or baste, sew together leaving opening at bottom to insert batting. Turn right side out. Insert batting.

7. Referring to photo, sew head to body with natural thread.

8. Make bow from ribbon. Sew as desired onto doll's head. Sew button onto center of bow.

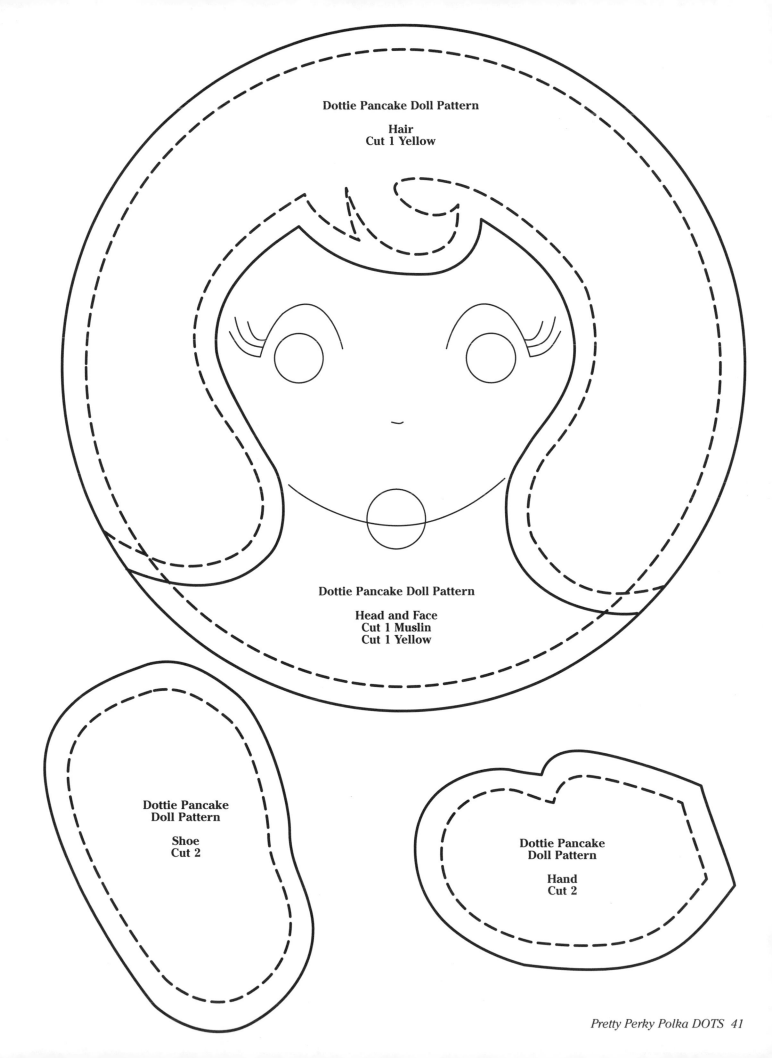

Dottie Pancake Doll Pattern

**Hair
Cut 1 Yellow**

Dottie Pancake Doll Pattern

**Head and Face
Cut 1 Muslin
Cut 1 Yellow**

**Dottie Pancake
Doll Pattern**

**Shoe
Cut 2**

**Dottie Pancake
Doll Pattern**

**Hand
Cut 2**

Aunt Dottie Mae Mammy Doll

Photo on page 13

FINISHED SIZE: 15$\frac{1}{2}$" tall

MATERIALS:
- $\frac{1}{8}$ yard of 44" wide of Black fabric
- $\frac{1}{2}$ yard of 44" wide of Red and White polka dot fabric
- $\frac{1}{8}$ yard of 44" wide of White fabric
- 26" of $\frac{1}{2}$" wide of White lace trim
- 1 yard of $\frac{1}{2}$" of Red bias binding
- 2 White $\frac{1}{2}$" buttons
- 2 White $\frac{1}{2}$" plastic rings
- Scrap of posterboard
- 5" piece of wooden dowel
- Red embroidery floss
- Polyester stuffing • pins • thread • needle • scissors

INSTRUCTIONS:

1. Use $\frac{1}{4}$" seam allowances throughout.

2. Cut the body, arm, bodice, apron straps, base and base cover according to the patterns on pages 42 and 43.

3. With right sides facing, sew 2 arm pieces together, leaving the end open. Turn to right side, stuff arm firmly. Pin or sew end closed. Repeat with other arm. Clip curves as necessary.

4. Embroider mouth on one body piece. Sew button eyes in place. With right sides facing, sew the body pieces together, leaving the arms and bottom open. Turn to right side. Insert dowel into body. Stuff head firmly. Fold back seam allowance at armholes. Insert an arm in each opening, thumbs up, and sew across armhole to secure arms. Stuff body firmly. Lay body aside.

5. Center base on wrong side of one piece of base cover fabric. Fold edges of fabric over edges of base. Fold back the seam allowance on remaining piece of the base cover. Lay that piece right side facing on top of base. Hand sew folded edges to the piece of fabric covering the base around all edges. Fold back seam allowance around bottom of doll and set doll on base. Sew through bottom edges of doll and base to attach doll firmly in place. Set doll aside.

Wrong side

6. Sew shoulder seam of bodice pieces, with right sides facing. Apply bias tape facing to neckline. For sleeves, cut 2 pieces of polka dot fabric 5$\frac{1}{2}$" x 6". Fold back $\frac{1}{8}$" twice on one 6" end, topstitch. Gather other 6" end to fit armhole on bodice. Pull gathers even, sew sleeve in place, right sides facing. Repeat with other sleeve. Sew underarm and side seams.

7. For skirt, cut a 27$\frac{1}{2}$" x 12" piece of polka dot fabric. Gather top raw edge to fit bottom of bodice. Pull gathers even and, with right sides facing, sew skirt to bodice, aligning raw edges. With right sides facing, sew ends of skirt together for back seam. Fold back $\frac{1}{8}$" twice around hem, topstitch. Place dress on doll. Fold back seam allowance one one side of bodice back, overlap folded edges over other side of bodice and hand sew seam closed. Gather each sleeve $\frac{1}{2}$" from end to fit wrists.

8. Sew a strip of seam tape down the center of 2 apron straps. Sew a plain strap to one of the straps with tape, right sides facing and leaving straight end open. Turn to right side and. Repeat with other strap. For apron, cut a piece of White fabric 12 x 7$\frac{1}{4}$". Fold back $\frac{1}{8}$" twice along each shorter edge and across bottom. Topstitch. Topstitch again to secure edge of lace to back of apron around the finished edges. Topstitch seam tape to apron front, placing it $\frac{1}{2}$" from finished edges.

Cut a 4$\frac{1}{2}$" x 2" waistband for apron from White fabric. Gather top raw edge of apron between ends of seam tape so top of apron measures 4". With right sides facing, sew apron front to waistband across one long raw edge. Align outer edges of lace with seam line at each end of waistband. Fold in seam allowance at each end of waistband. Cut 2 White apron ties 11$\frac{1}{2}$" x 1$\frac{1}{2}$". With right sides facing, sew across end and down long edges, leaving end open. Turn to right side.

Fold each open end in a pleat to measure $\frac{1}{2}$" across. Baste or pin ends of ties at either end of waistband. Fold down seam allowance across top edge of apron. Overlap open ends of apron straps at center of waistband top. Fold waistband down to overlap gathers of apron. Topstitch across ends and gathers. Place apron on doll, pull straps over shoulders to overlap at the back over the waist and tie apron ties in a bow.

Aunt Dottie Mae Doll
Body
Cut 1
Black fabric
Reverse
Cut 1

Wrong side

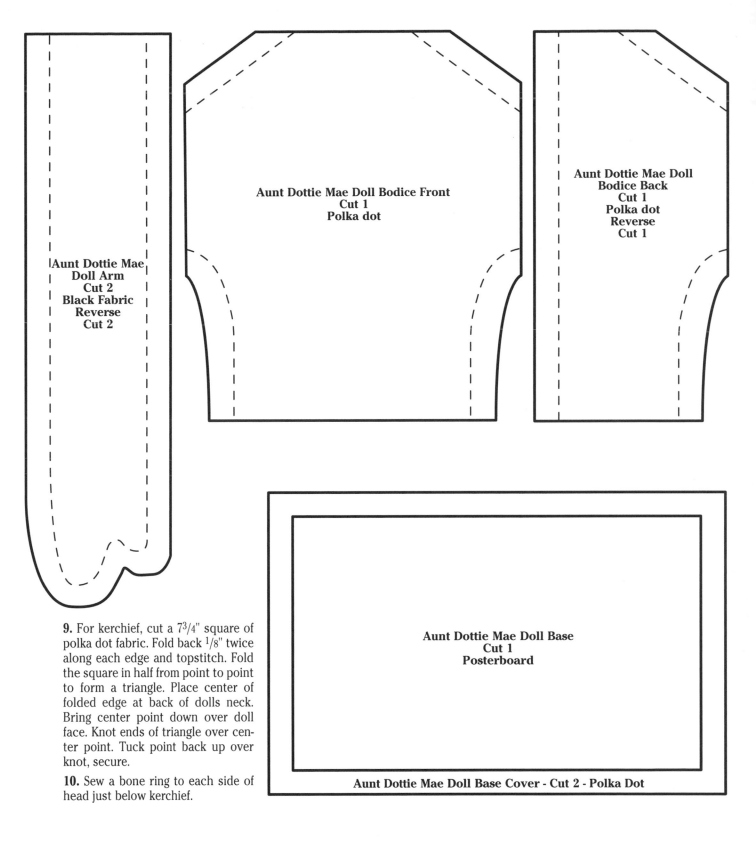

Aunt Dottie Mae
Doll Arm
Cut 2
Black Fabric
Reverse
Cut 2

Aunt Dottie Mae Doll Bodice Front
Cut 1
Polka dot

Aunt Dottie Mae Doll
Bodice Back
Cut 1
Polka dot
Reverse
Cut 1

Aunt Dottie Mae Doll Base
Cut 1
Posterboard

Aunt Dottie Mae Doll Base Cover - Cut 2 - Polka Dot

9. For kerchief, cut a 7³/₄" square of polka dot fabric. Fold back ¹/₈" twice along each edge and topstitch. Fold the square in half from point to point to form a triangle. Place center of folded edge at back of dolls neck. Bring center point down over doll face. Knot ends of triangle over center point. Tuck point back up over knot, secure.

10. Sew a bone ring to each side of head just below kerchief.

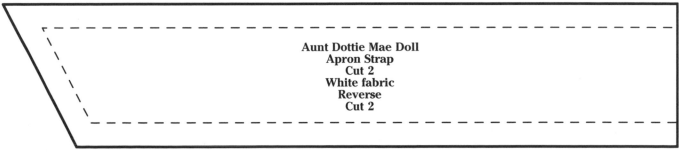

Aunt Dottie Mae Doll
Apron Strap
Cut 2
White fabric
Reverse
Cut 2

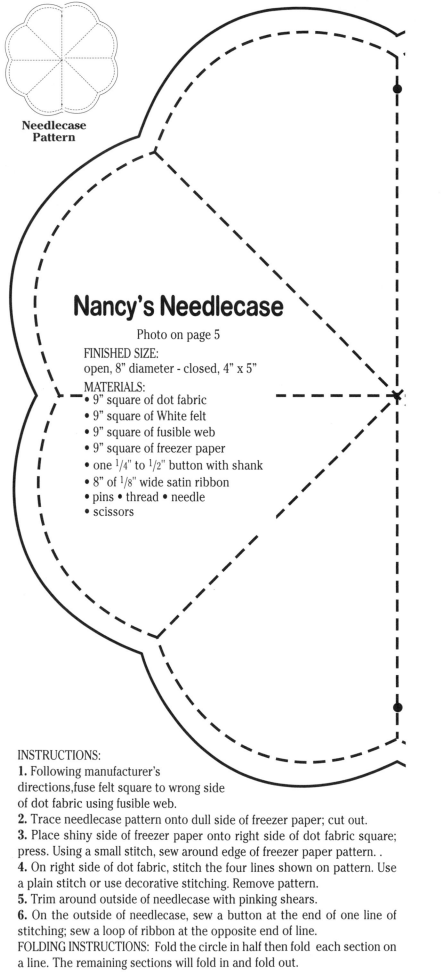

Nancy's Needlecase

Photo on page 5

FINISHED SIZE:
open, 8" diameter - closed, 4" x 5"

MATERIALS:
- 9" square of dot fabric
- 9" square of White felt
- 9" square of fusible web
- 9" square of freezer paper
- one $1/4$" to $1/2$" button with shank
- 8" of $1/8$" wide satin ribbon
- pins • thread • needle
- scissors

INSTRUCTIONS:
1. Following manufacturer's directions, fuse felt square to wrong side of dot fabric using fusible web.
2. Trace needlecase pattern onto dull side of freezer paper; cut out.
3. Place shiny side of freezer paper onto right side of dot fabric square; press. Using a small stitch, sew around edge of freezer paper pattern. .
4. On right side of dot fabric, stitch the four lines shown on pattern. Use a plain stitch or use decorative stitching. Remove pattern.
5. Trim around outside of needlecase with pinking shears.
6. On the outside of needlecase, sew a button at the end of one line of stitching; sew a loop of ribbon at the opposite end of line.

FOLDING INSTRUCTIONS: Fold the circle in half then fold each section on a line. The remaining sections will fold in and fold out. Press flat.

Naughty Puppies Apron

Photo on page 11

FINISHED SIZE:
14 $3/4$" long x 16 $3/4$" wide

MATERIALS:
- $3/4$ yard of muslin fabric
- 3 $1/2$ yards of $1/4$" Red polka dot double fold bias binding (optional, make your own)
- Red embroidery floss
- pins • thread • needle
- scissors

TIP: Embroider the design before the pattern piece is cut out.

INSTRUCTIONS:

1. Cut muslin into two 24" x 36" panels. Trace "puppies" design onto one panel referring to photo for placement. Stitch design using a Straight Stitch for the puppies' hair and a Stem Stitch for their eyes, chins, feet and for all other lines in the design.

2. For front panel, cut rounded pocket curves from embroidered panel (see illustration).

3. Sew bias tape around the pocket curves of front panel.

4. Align the two pattern pieces. Fold bias tape around the side and bottom edges, encasing both panels. Pin in place and sew bias tape to all layers.

5. Cut 45" of bias tape for ties. Center the tape on the top edge of apron. Enclose edge with tape. Pin in place across entire length of top edge. Sew along entire length of bias tape. Knot the ends of tape, or finish by turning raw edges to the inside and stitch closed.

6 3/4" 3 1/2" 6 3/4"

6"

15"

Red and White Hankies Apron

Photo on page 11

FINISHED SIZE:

18" long x 28"wide

MATERIALS:

• Four matching 12" square hankies
• 51" of White 1 1/2" wide satin ribbon
• Optional: 1/4 yard polka dot fabric
• pins • thread • needles • scissors

TIP: Use 1/4" seam allowances throughout.

INSTRUCTIONS:

1. For the pocket panel, fold one hankie in half, right sides facing. Fold down top corners to meet at center front. Sew down center edge of each pocket. Press folds.

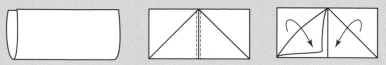

2. For the bottom panels, press pleats in 2 hankies as shown in the illustration. For symmetrical pleats turn one napkin upside down and baste the pleats in place across the top edges. With right sides facing, sew the pleated napkins together down the center. Press the seam open. With right sides facing, sew the basted pleats across the bottom fold of the pocket panel.

3. For the apron sides, cut the remaining napkin in half diagonally. With right sides facing, sew each triangle to a side of the pleated & pocket panels. Press the seam open.

4. Locate the center of the ribbon. Align it with the center of the pocket panel. With right sides facing, sew the ribbon across the top of the apron. Press the seam down. Trim each ribbon end at a 45° angle.

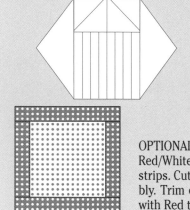

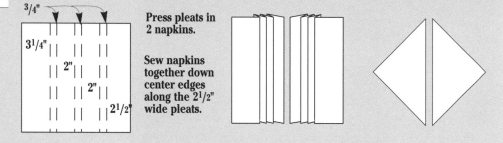

Press pleats in 2 napkins.

Sew napkins together down center edges along the 2 1/2" wide pleats.

OPTIONAL: To make your own hankie squares, cut 4 White/Red 9 1/2" squares. Cut 8 Red/White 2 1/4" x 9 1/2" Red/White strips. Sew a strip at either side of each square. Trim ends even. Press seams toward Red strips. Cut 8 Red/White 2 1/4" x 12 1/2" strips. Sew a strip to the top and bottom of each square/strip assembly. Trim ends even. Press seams toward Red strips. Finish edges by turning back 1/8" twice. Topstitch with Red thread.

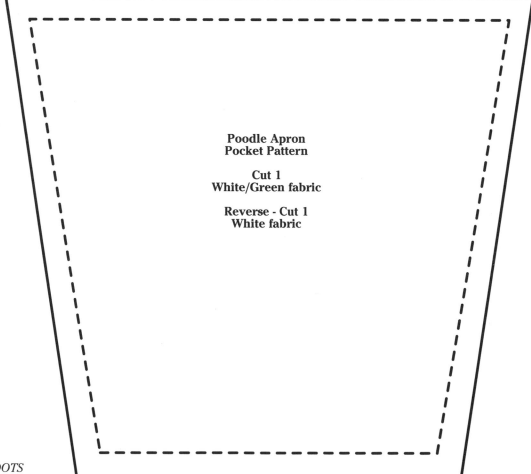

Poodle Apron
Pocket Pattern

Cut 1
White/Green fabric

Reverse - Cut 1
White fabric

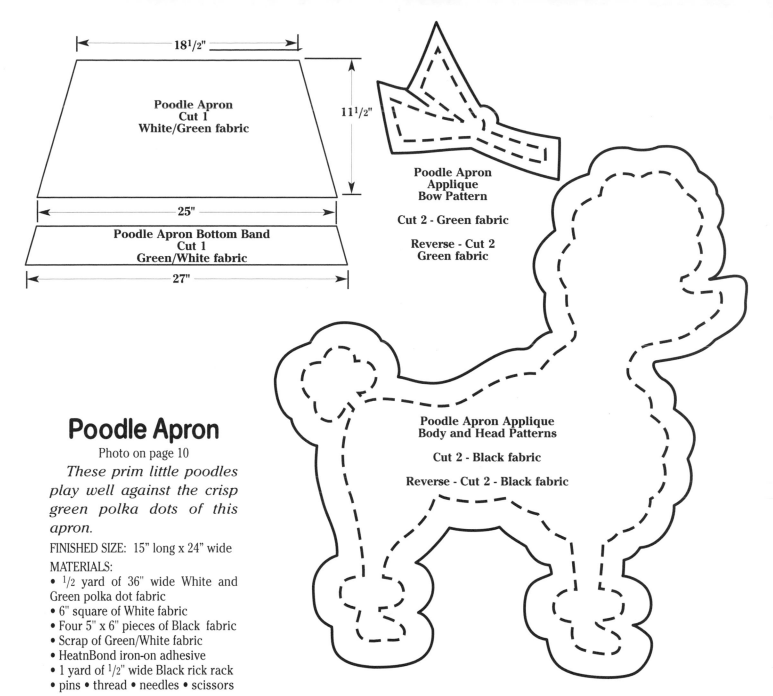

18¹/₂"

Poodle Apron
Cut 1
White/Green fabric

11¹/₂"

25"

Poodle Apron Bottom Band
Cut 1
Green/White fabric

27"

Poodle Apron
Applique
Bow Pattern

Cut 2 - Green fabric

Reverse - Cut 2
Green fabric

Poodle Apron Applique
Body and Head Patterns

Cut 2 - Black fabric

Reverse - Cut 2 - Black fabric

Poodle Apron

Photo on page 10

These prim little poodles play well against the crisp green polka dots of this apron.

FINISHED SIZE: 15" long x 24" wide

MATERIALS:

• ¹/₂ yard of 36" wide White and Green polka dot fabric
• 6" square of White fabric
• Four 5" x 6" pieces of Black fabric
• Scrap of Green/White fabric
• HeatnBond iron-on adhesive
• 1 yard of ¹/₂" wide Black rick rack
• pins • thread • needles • scissors

TIP: Use ¹/₄" seam allowances throughout.

INSTRUCTIONS:

1. For the apron, cut a 11¹/₂" x 25" piece of White/Green fabric as shown in the cutting diagram. For the bottom apron strip, cut a 3¹/₄" x 27" strip of Green White fabric as shown. For the pocket, cut a 6" piece each of White/Green and White fabric

2. With right sides facing and matching edges aligned, sew the bottom strip to the bottom of the apron. Press the seam down. Use Black thread to sew rick rack over the seam, trim ends even with apron edges. Finish the side and bottom edges of the apron by folding back ¹/₄" twice, topstitch with White thread.

3. For the waistband, cut a strip of Green/White fabric 2¹/₂" x 55" (piece if necessary). Iron ¹/₄" seam allowances on all edges. With right sides facing, align center of apron with center of

waistband. Sew waistband to apron. Fold waistband together lengthwise, wrong sides together. Topstitch all around.

4. For pocket, hold White/Green and White fabric together, right sides facing. Sew pieces together, leaving an opening along one side for turning. Turn to right side, sew opening closed. Press pocket. With Black thread, sew a piece of rick rack across the pocket 1" below the top edge. Fold ¹/₄" of rick rack at each end to back of pocket. Attach pocket to apron as desired, topstitch in place. Reinforce top corners with additional topstitching.

5. Following the manufacturer's instructions for iron-on adhesives, bond to black and green fabrics. Cut 2 Black poodles, reverse and cut 2 more. Cut 2 Green bows, reverse and cut 2 more. Attach poodles and bows to the front of the apron.

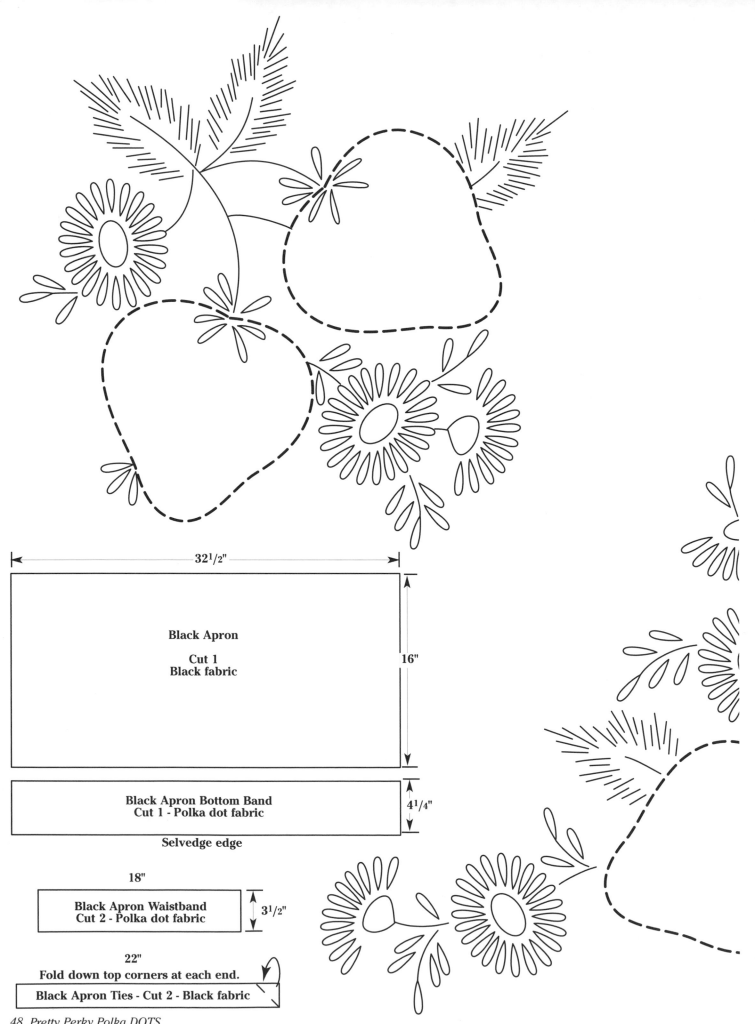

Black Apron

Cut 1
Black fabric

32¹/₂"

16"

Black Apron Bottom Band
Cut 1 - Polka dot fabric

4¹/₄"

Selvedge edge

18"

Black Apron Waistband
Cut 2 - Polka dot fabric

3¹/₂"

22"

Fold down top corners at each end.

Black Apron Ties - Cut 2 - Black fabric

Black Apron with Strawberries

Photo on page 10

Feisty red strawberries on a black field entice you to play.

FINISHED SIZE: 21" long x 31" wide

MATERIALS:
- 3/4 yard of 36" wide Black fabric
- 1/4 yard of 36" wide Red and White dot fabric
- White, Gold, Green and Variegated Green embroidery flosses
- White transfer pencil
- pins • thread • needles • scissors

TIP: Use 1/4" seam allowances throughout.

INSTRUCTIONS:

1 For the apron, cut a 32½" x 16" piece of Black fabric. For the ties, cut two 22" x 2" strips of Black fabric. For the waistband, cut one 3½" x 18" pieces of polka dot fabric. For apron bottom cut one 32½" x 4¼" piece of polka dot fabric, placing one long edge along the selvedge edge of the fabric. (Note: This will eliminate having to finish the lower edge of the strip.)

2 Transfer the embroidery patterns to the Black fabric. Embroider designs. Applique polka dot strawberries in place.

3. With right sides facing and with raw edges aligned, sew the 32½" polka dot strip across the bottom of the apron. Press seam toward the bottom strip. Turn side edges 1/8" twice, topstitch.

4. Working 1/4" below the top raw edge of the apron, gather the top edge to 16" wide. Distribute gathers evenly and secure the thread ends.

5. Attach waistband to apron body by laying right sides facing along top edge of apron. Stitch across top edge, making sure to cover the gathering stitches. Fold under 1/4" along the remaining long edge of band, press. Fold waistband in half to wrong side of apron and pin in place. Topstitch waistband in place. Tuck in raw edges of waistband and press.

6. Insert tie in waistband, tucking to fit. Topstitch along folded edge of waistband.

Pantaloons Apron

Photo on page 10

FINISHED SIZE: 18" long x 32" wide

MATERIALS:
• 1 yard of 36" wide dot fabric
• pins • thread • needles • scissors

TIP: Use $1/4$" seam allowances throughout.

INSTRUCTIONS:

1. For the apron, cut a 33" x 22" piece of fabric. At the bottom cut a 5" wide x 7" high opening with a rounded top edge in the center of the bottom edge, as shown on the illustration. To finish the edges, fold back $1/8$" twice and topstitch.

2. Finish the side edges of the apron by folding back $1/8$" twice, top stitch. Repeat to finish the lower edge of each leg.

3. Beginning $1 1/4$" above the leg edge, gather the leg to measure $7 1/2$" across. Pull gathers even. Secure thread ends. Repeat to make another row of gathering stitches $1/2$" above the first row. Repeat for the other leg.

4. Working $1/4$" below the top raw edge of the apron, gather the top edge to 16" wide. Pull gathers even and secure the thread ends.

5. For the waistband/ties, cut two $3 1/2$" wide pieces of fabric from one selvedge edge to the other across the fabric. (Note: This will eliminate having to finish the ends of the ties.) With right sides facing, sew the two raw ends together. Press seam open.

Locate the center of the apron, align with the center seam on the waistband. With right sides facing, and raw edges even, sew the front of the waistband to the top of the apron. Fold back $1/4$" along the back raw edge of the waistband across the center 17". Fold the waistband in half and pin in place, with back edge aligned with the stitched edge of the waistband. Begin $1/2$" beyond the edge of the apron to topstitch through all layers to $1/2$" beyond the other edge.

Finish the remaining raw edges of the ties by folding back $1/8$" twice along each edge. Topstitch.

Aqua Apron with Rick Rack

Photo on page 11

This pretty pastel apron will brighten your time spent in the kitchen.

FINISHED SIZE: 17" long x 28" wide

MATERIALS:
1 yard of 36" wide dot fabric
• 3 yards of $1/2$" wide White rick rack
• pins • thread • needles • scissors

TIP: Use $1/4$" seam allowances.

CUTTING:
• Cut one 17" x 30" piece of fabric for the apron as shown on pattern
• Cut one 14" x 17" piece
• Waistband: Cut one 4" x 28" piece
• Ties: Cut two 3" x 24" strips of fabric.

INSTRUCTIONS:

1. Finish the side and bottom edges of apron and pocket panel by folding under $1/4$" twice, topstitch. Sew rick rack around the sides and pointed edges of pocket panel.

2. Align center of apron with center of pocket panel. Baste or pin the top edges together. Sew through all layers along pointed edge of panel to attach it to the apron. Also, sew through all layers down the center of panel to separate the pockets. Sew rick rack along remaining points and sides of apron.

3. Align center of top edge of apron with center of waistband. With right sides facing, and raw edges even, sew front of waistband to top of the apron. Fold under $1/4$" along the back raw edge and sides of waistband. Fold waistband in half and pin in place, with back edge aligned slightly below the front edge of the waistband. Topstitch through all layers to sew the bottom closed and to finish attaching waistband to apron. Do not sew the ends closed.

4. Finish the long raw edges of the ties by folding back $1/4$" twice along each edge. Topstitch. Fold a lengthwise pleat at the raw edge of one tie so it is almost as wide as waistband. Insert the end into waistband and topstitch the waistband end closed. Repeat with the other tie.

Illustrations of patterns on page 51

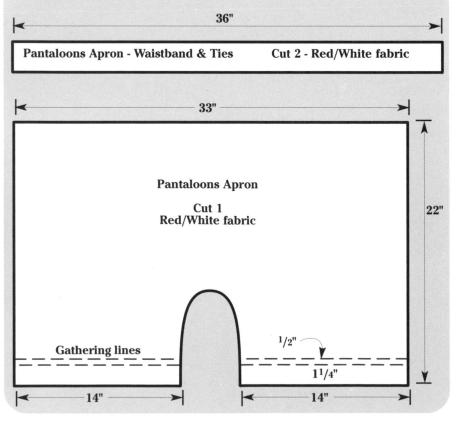

36"

| Pantaloons Apron - Waistband & Ties | Cut 2 - Red/White fabric |

33"

Pantaloons Apron

**Cut 1
Red/White fabric**

22"

Gathering lines

1/2"

$1 1/4$"

14"   14"

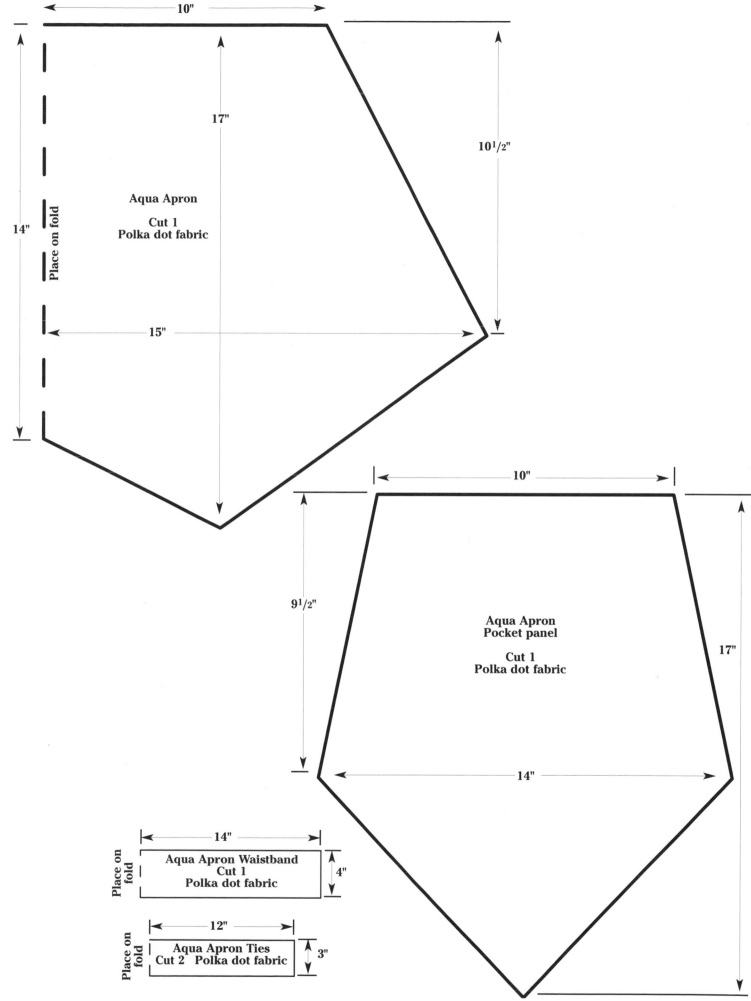

10"

17"

10¹/₂"

14"

Place on fold

Aqua Apron

Cut 1
Polka dot fabric

15"

10"

9¹/₂"

17"

Aqua Apron
Pocket panel

Cut 1
Polka dot fabric

14"

14"

Place on fold

Aqua Apron Waistband
Cut 1
Polka dot fabric

4"

12"

Place on fold

Aqua Apron Ties
Cut 2 Polka dot fabric

3"

Needlework Quilt

Photo on page 5

FINISHED SIZE: $20^1/2$" x $28^1/2$"

TIP: Embroider blocks before cutting apart.

MATERIALS:
- $^1/2$ yard White fabric
- $^1/6$ yard of Red check fabric
- $^3/4$ yard of Red dot fabric
- $^2/3$ yard backing fabric
- Red embroidery floss
- pins • thread • needles • scissors

TIP: Use $^1/4$" seam allowances throughout.

Needlework Quilt Pattern

**Small Squares
for 4-Patch Blocks**

**Cut 28 Red Dot
Cut 28 Check**

Needlework Quilt Pattern

**Scallops
Cut 48 Red Dot**

Needlework Quilt Pattern

**Cut 4 Red Dot
Cut 17 White**

NEEDLE

WORK

INSTRUCTIONS:

1. Cut 2 strips $2^1/4$" x 36" of one Red dot fabric; cut 2 strips $2^1/4$" x 36" Red check fabric. Sew strips together on the long edge. Cut the joined fabric into 28 strips $2^1/4$" wide.

2. Create 14 blocks by sewing two $2^1/4$" strips together, alternating patterns.

3. Cut four 4" squares from the Red dot fabric. Fold same fabric, right sides together, to make scallops. Draw scallops across fabric. Cut apart, do not cut around design. Stitch 1/4" inside curved edge only. Trim curved edge with sharp scissors. Using pinking shears $^1/8$" to $^3/16$" from stitching line makes scallop easier to turn and lays better. Turn right side out; press.

4. Mark squares and copy the 17 designs onto White fabric. Embroider with Red floss. Sew blocks together as shown.

5. With curves toward center, lay 7 scallops on long edges of quilt top and 5 scallops on short edges, align straight sides with edges of top. Leave $^1/4$" at each end of quilt edge to facilitate turning corners. Pin or baste in place.

6. Sandwich quilt top, backing and batting as follows: lay quilt top facing up (scallops laying toward center of top). Lay backing, right side facing front of quilt top. Lay batting on top of backing fabric. Pin or baste around edges. Sew $^1/4$" from raw edge of all layers, leaving a 6" to 8" opening in the middle of one edge; turn right side out. Blind stitch opening closed.

7. Quilt around all White blocks with Red thread if desired.

Patterns continued on pages 52-53

Scottie Dogs Quilt

Photo on page 4

FINISHED SIZE: 47" x 57"

MATERIALS:
- $1/4$ yard of Navy on White dots fabric for dogs
- $1/4$ yard of White on Navy dots fabric for dogs
- $1/4$ yard each of assorted fabrics, for squares and dog coats
- $1 1/3$ yard of a light-colored plaid fabric for background
- $1 2/3$ yards of fabric for backing
- 7 yards of $3/8$" double fold Red bias binding
- $2 2/3$ yards of $3/4$" wide dot ribbon - Cut sixteen 6" pieces for bows
- 16 Red $3/8$" buttons for eyes
- 20 Red $7/8$" buttons
- Quilt batting
- pins • thread • needles • scissors

TIP: Use $1/4$" seam allowances throughout.

CUTTING:
Cut 39 strips $2 1/2$" x 18" (to make squares for border)

TIP: First, sew $2 1/2$" long strips together (3 assorted fabrics in each strip).
Next, cut strips into $2 1/2$" widths (3 fabrics in each). Rearrange widths in a random fashion.
Sew together (step 2).

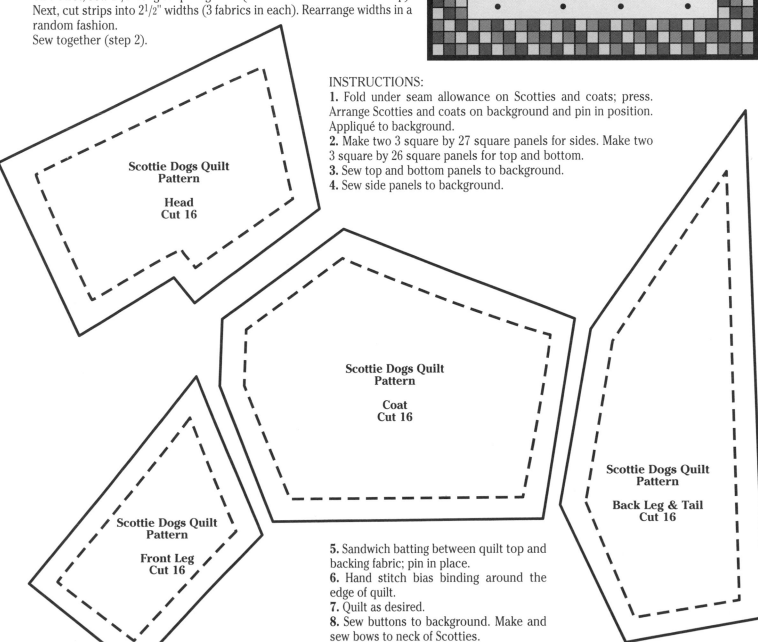

INSTRUCTIONS:
1. Fold under seam allowance on Scotties and coats; press. Arrange Scotties and coats on background and pin in position. Appliqué to background.
2. Make two 3 square by 27 square panels for sides. Make two 3 square by 26 square panels for top and bottom.
3. Sew top and bottom panels to background.
4. Sew side panels to background.

Scottie Dogs Quilt Pattern

Head Cut 16

Scottie Dogs Quilt Pattern

Coat Cut 16

Scottie Dogs Quilt Pattern

Back Leg & Tail Cut 16

Scottie Dogs Quilt Pattern

Front Leg Cut 16

5. Sandwich batting between quilt top and backing fabric; pin in place.
6. Hand stitch bias binding around the edge of quilt.
7. Quilt as desired.
8. Sew buttons to background. Make and sew bows to neck of Scotties.

Blue Floral

Photo on page 6

TIP: Add a 1/4" seam to all applique patterns. Turn seams under and press before stitching. Secure to the background with a Blind Stitch.

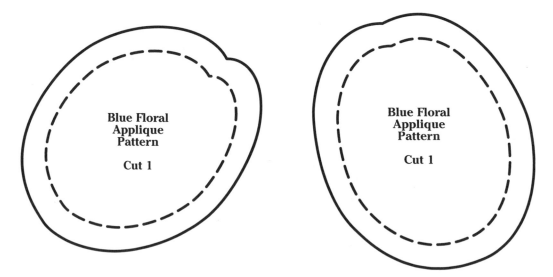

Blue Floral
Applique
Pattern

Cut 1

Blue Floral
Applique
Pattern

Cut 1

Country Girl

Photo on page 6

TIP: Add a ¼" seam to all applique patterns. Turn seams under and press before stitching. Secure to the background with a Blind Stitch.

TINTING: Tint goose, chickens and arms with crayons (see page 96).

RUFFLE: Handstitch an 8" long piece of ¾" wide gathered eyelet lace on the bottom of the skirt for a ruffle.

Country Girl
Applique Pattern

Skirt
Cut 1

Bonnet
Cut 1

Dancing Plates

Photo on page 6

TIP: Add a ¼" seam to all applique patterns. Turn seams under and press before stitching. Secure to the background with a Blind Stitch.

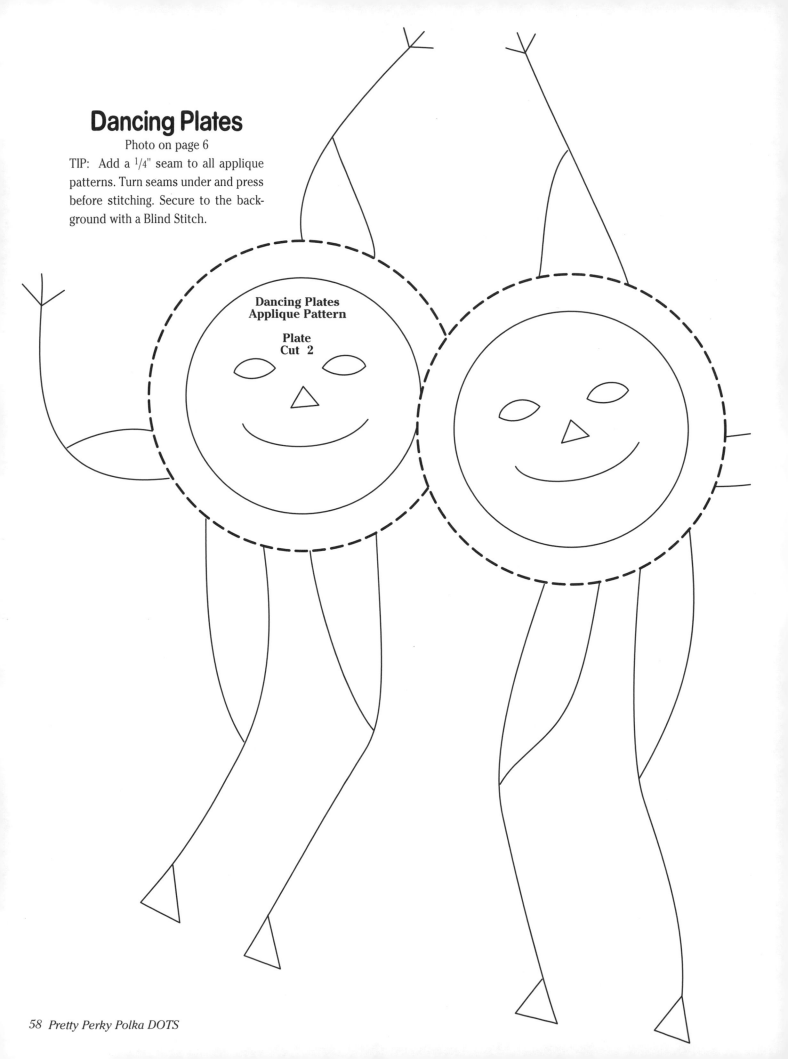

Dancing Plates Applique Pattern

Plate Cut 2

Polka Dot Trivia

The DOT is the oldest piece of art known to mankind! It originally may not have been planned to be just that, but the accidental meeting of a piece of charcoal or graphite on a white slab of stone, marked what is known as a dot.

DOTS found their way to textiles by providing a background to early designs such as fruits and flowers. Picotage is a small dotted background found on early chintz furnishing fabrics. Civil War era quilts show many fabrics of different size dots, particularly in the wilder prints of the day, some even presented in a whimsical fashion. Turn of the Century dots printed in many of the resist Indigos were dominant. The mourning black and white prints of Queen Victoria's realm, certainly used dots alone, or with other designs. These dot prints were two color therefore inexpensive.

A DOT is round and solid in color, not to be confused with a circle, which is open or has a motif inside. Dots that go berserk, or look like thrown confetti, are referred to as "spotted" cotton.

Most Polka Dots are even spaced, no matter what size.

Oversize dots are referred to as "coin size".

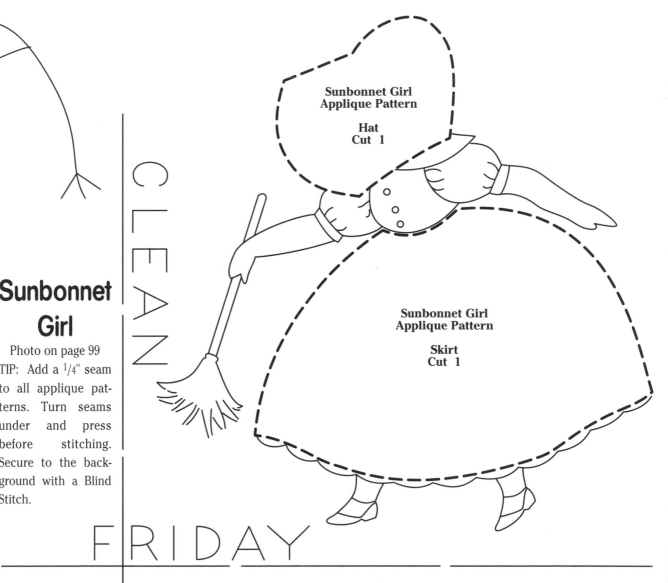

Sunbonnet Girl

Photo on page 99

TIP: Add a $1/4$" seam to all applique patterns. Turn seams under and press before stitching. Secure to the background with a Blind Stitch.

Sunbonnet Girl
Applique Pattern

Hat
Cut 1

Sunbonnet Girl
Applique Pattern

Skirt
Cut 1

C L E A N

F R I D A Y

Boy Meets Girl

Photo on page 7

TIP: Add a $1/4$" seam to all applique patterns. Turn seams under and press before stitching. Secure to the background with a Blind Stitch.

Hat Cut 1

Applique Pattern Coat Cut 1

Boy Meets Girl Applique Pattern Pants Cut 1

Boy Meets Girl
Applique
Pattern

Apron
Cut 1

Boy Meets Girl
Applique
Pattern

Dress
Cut 1

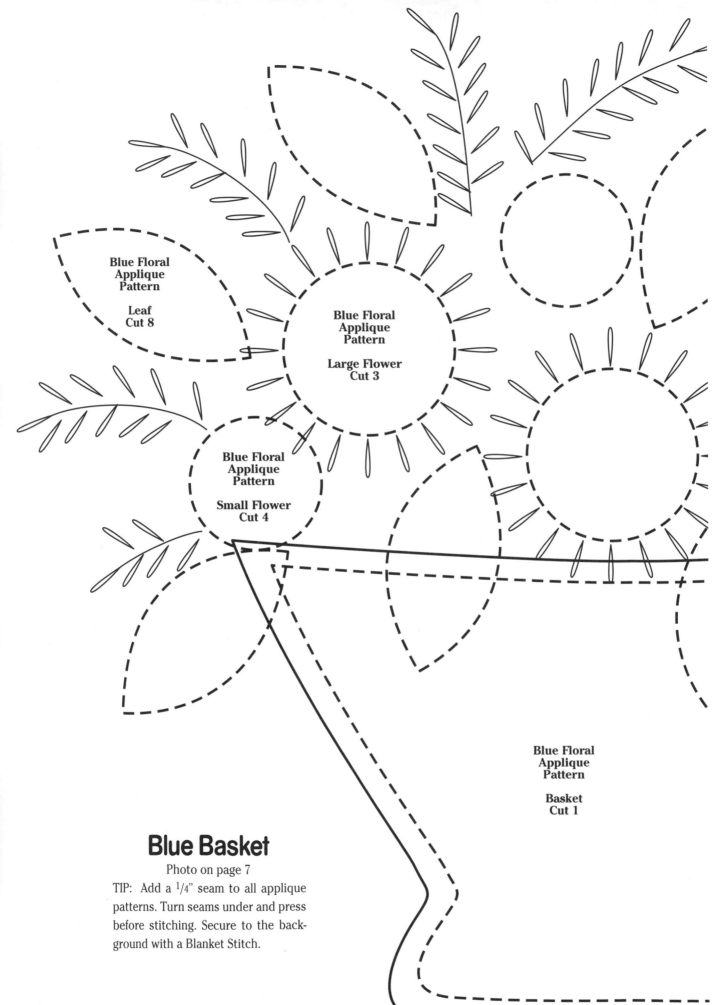

Blue Floral Applique Pattern

Leaf
Cut 8

Blue Floral Applique Pattern

Large Flower
Cut 3

Blue Floral Applique Pattern

Small Flower
Cut 4

Blue Floral Applique Pattern

Basket
Cut 1

Blue Basket

Photo on page 7

TIP: Add a $1/4$" seam to all applique patterns. Turn seams under and press before stitching. Secure to the background with a Blanket Stitch.

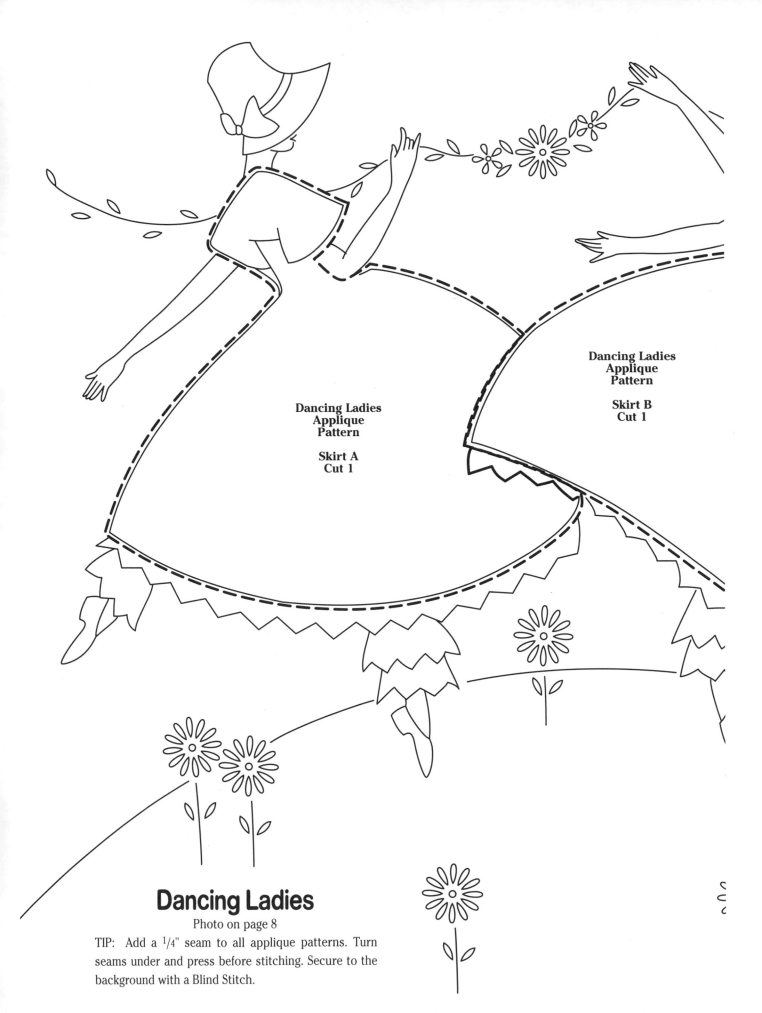

Dancing Ladies
Applique
Pattern

Skirt A
Cut 1

Dancing Ladies
Applique
Pattern

Skirt B
Cut 1

Dancing Ladies

Photo on page 8

TIP: Add a 1/4" seam to all applique patterns. Turn
seams under and press before stitching. Secure to the
background with a Blind Stitch.

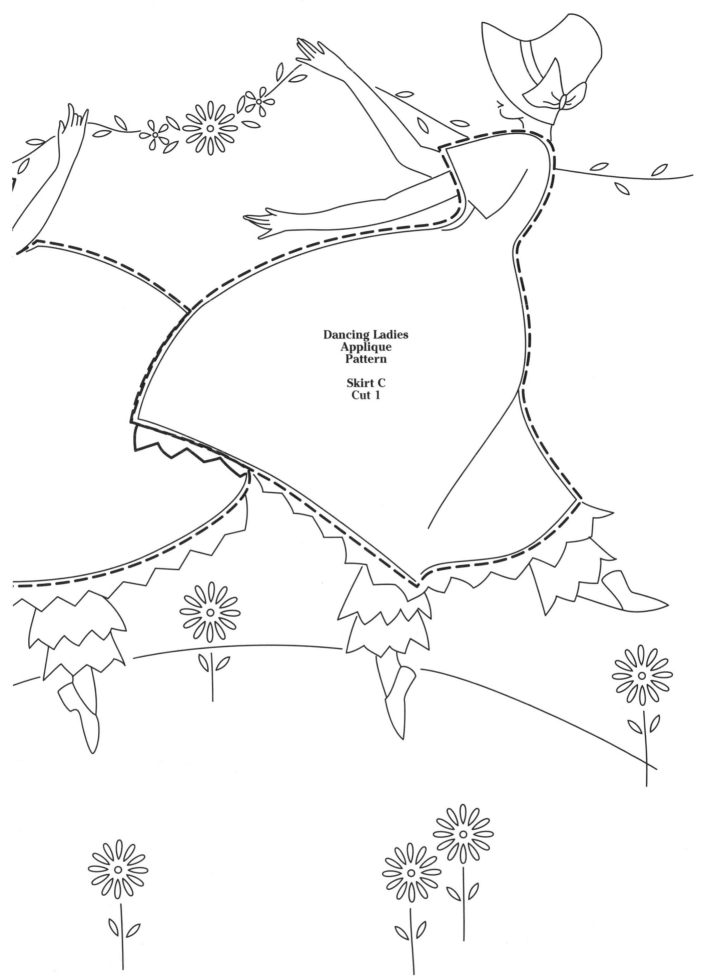

Dancing Ladies
Applique
Pattern

Skirt C
Cut 1

Pink Lady

Photo on page 8

TIP: Add a $1/4$" seam to all applique patterns. Turn seams under and press before stitching. Secure to the background with a Blanket Stitch.

Pink Lady
Applique
Pattern

Skirt A
Cut 1

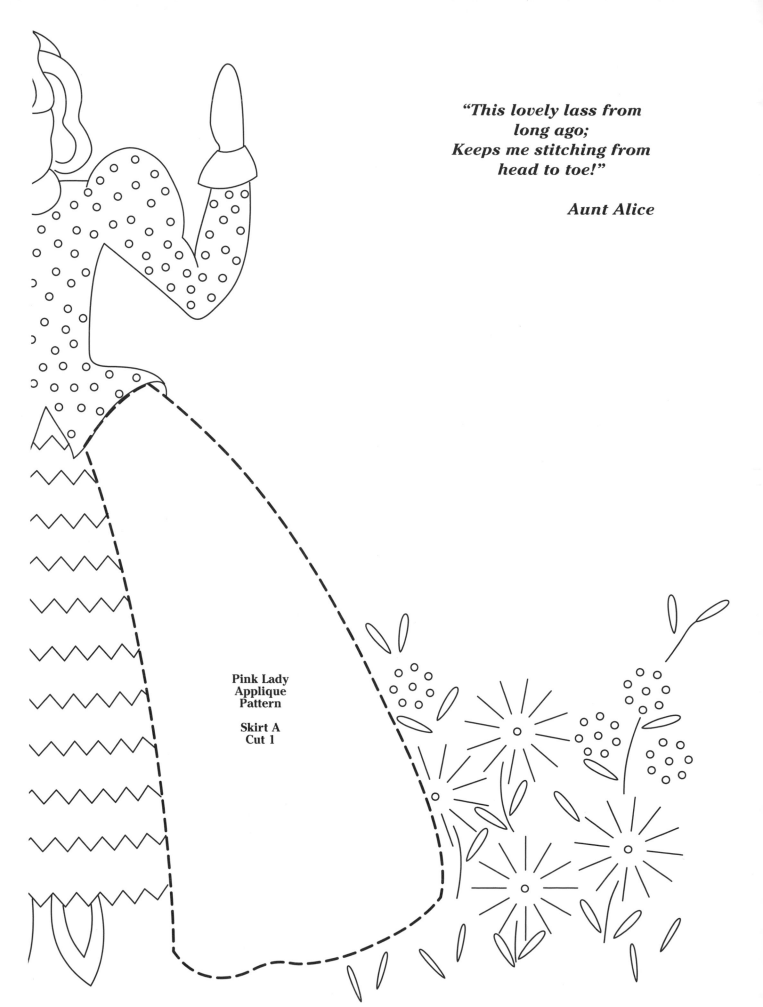

"This lovely lass from long ago;
Keeps me stitching from head to toe!"

Aunt Alice

**Pink Lady
Applique
Pattern**

**Skirt A
Cut 1**

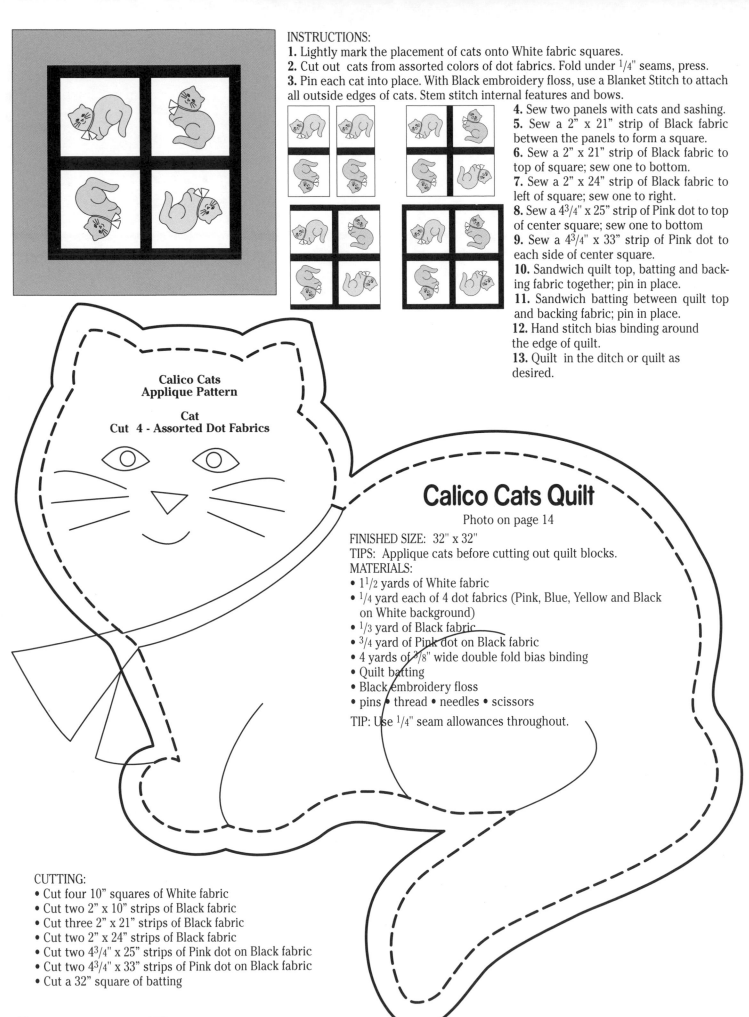

INSTRUCTIONS:

1. Lightly mark the placement of cats onto White fabric squares.
2. Cut out cats from assorted colors of dot fabrics. Fold under ¹/₄" seams, press.
3. Pin each cat into place. With Black embroidery floss, use a Blanket Stitch to attach all outside edges of cats. Stem stitch internal features and bows.
4. Sew two panels with cats and sashing.
5. Sew a 2" x 21" strip of Black fabric between the panels to form a square.
6. Sew a 2" x 21" strip of Black fabric to top of square; sew one to bottom.
7. Sew a 2" x 24" strip of Black fabric to left of square; sew one to right.
8. Sew a 4³/₄" x 25" strip of Pink dot to top of center square; sew one to bottom
9. Sew a 4³/₄" x 33" strip of Pink dot to each side of center square.
10. Sandwich quilt top, batting and backing fabric together; pin in place.
11. Sandwich batting between quilt top and backing fabric; pin in place.
12. Hand stitch bias binding around the edge of quilt.
13. Quilt in the ditch or quilt as desired.

Calico Cats
Applique Pattern

Cat
Cut 4 - Assorted Dot Fabrics

Calico Cats Quilt

Photo on page 14

FINISHED SIZE: 32" x 32"
TIPS: Applique cats before cutting out quilt blocks.
MATERIALS:
• 1¹/₂ yards of White fabric
• ¹/₄ yard each of 4 dot fabrics (Pink, Blue, Yellow and Black on White background)
• ¹/₃ yard of Black fabric
• ³/₄ yard of Pink dot on Black fabric
• 4 yards of ³/₈" wide double fold bias binding
• Quilt batting
• Black embroidery floss
• pins • thread • needles • scissors

TIP: Use ¹/₄" seam allowances throughout.

CUTTING:
• Cut four 10" squares of White fabric
• Cut two 2" x 10" strips of Black fabric
• Cut three 2" x 21" strips of Black fabric
• Cut two 2" x 24" strips of Black fabric
• Cut two 4³/₄" x 25" strips of Pink dot on Black fabric
• Cut two 4³/₄" x 33" strips of Pink dot on Black fabric
• Cut a 32" square of batting

Ann's Dots Quilt

Photo on page 8

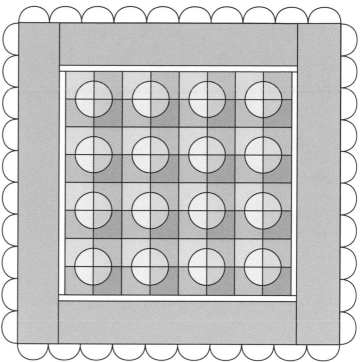

FINISHED SIZE: 34" x 34"

MATERIALS:
- $1/4$ yard each of 7 White dot on pastel fabrics
- $1^1/2$ yards of White fabric
  $3/4$ yard pattern B (wedge) - $3/4$ yard pattern C (scallop)
- 1 yard of Lavender fabric
- 1 yard of backing fabric
- $3/4$ yard of White fusible web
- Quilt batting
- pins • thread • needles • scissors

CUTTING:
- Cut 64 squares from assorted color dot fabrics, A
- Cut 64 White wedges, B
  (If using fusible web, omit seam allowance on curved edge)
- Cut 80 White scallops, C (fold fabric, right sides together)
- Cut two $1^1/4$" x 22" White strips • Cut two $1^1/4$" x 24" White strips
- Cut two $4^1/4$" x 25" Lavender strips
- Cut two $4^1/4$" x 31" Lavender strips
- Cut one $34^1/2$" x $34^1/2$" of backing fabric
- Cut a 34" square of quilt batting

TIP: Use $1/4$" seam allowances throughout.

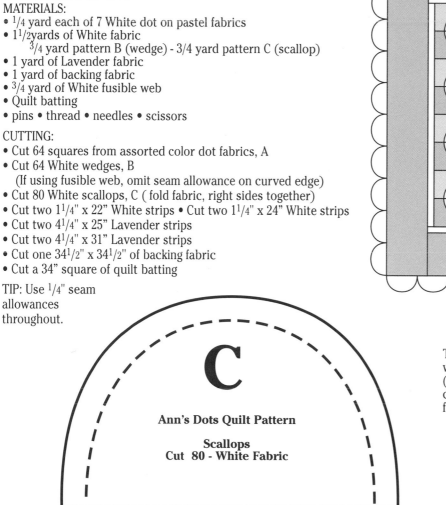

C

Ann's Dots Quilt Pattern

Scallops
Cut 80 - White Fabric

TIP: If using fusible web, fuse to pattern B (White fabric) before cutting. Follow manufacturer's directions.

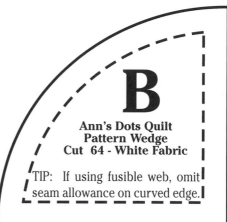

B

Ann's Dots Quilt Pattern Wedge Cut 64 - White Fabric

TIP: If using fusible web, omit seam allowance on curved edge.

INSTRUCTIONS:
1. Applique or fuse a White wedge to one corner of each $3^1/2$" square.
2. Sew 4 squares together, with wedges forming circles in the centers. Repeat 15 more times until you have 16 blocks.
3. Arrange in the order you prefer. Sew 4 blocks together into one strip. Repeat 3 more times.
4. Sew the 4 strips together to make the center square of quilt.
5. Sew a $1^1/4$" x 22" White strip to the left edge of center square. Repeat on right edge. Sew a $1^1/4$" x 24" White strip to top and bottom edges.
6. Sew a $4^1/4$" x 26" Lavender strip to left edge. Repeat on right edge. Sew a $4^1/4$" x 31" Lavender strip to top and bottom edges. Quilt front is complete.
7. Scallops: With fabric pinned right sides together, draw pattern C across fabric. Stitch scallop curve. Cut out. Use pinking shears to cut $1/8$" from stitching line to make curve lay better. Turn right side out; press.
8. With curves toward center, lay 10 scallops along one edge of quilt top, align straight sides with edge. Leave $1/4$" at each end of quilt edge to facilitate turning corners. Pin in place. Repeat on remaining edges.
9. Sandwich quilt top, backing and batting as follows: lay quilt top facing up (scallops laying toward center of top). Lay backing, right side facing front of quilt top. Lay batting on top of backing fabric. Pin around edges. Sew $1/4$" from raw edge of all layers, leaving a 6" to 8" opening in the middle of one edge. Turn right side out. Blind stitch opening closed.
10. Quilt as desired.

A

Ann's Dots Quilt Pattern

Square
Cut 64
Assorted Dot Fabrics

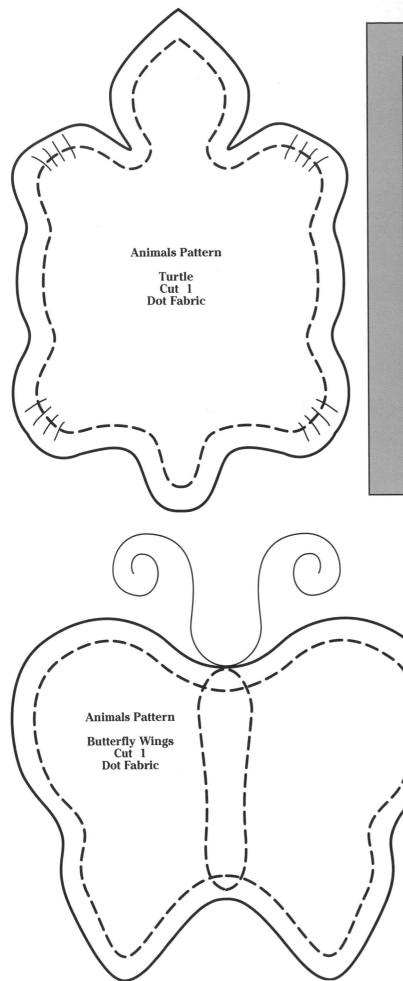

Animals Pattern

Turtle
Cut 1
Dot Fabric

Animals Pattern

Butterfly Wings
Cut 1
Dot Fabric

Favorite Animals Quilt

Photo on page 9

FINISHED SIZE: 29" x 39"

MATERIALS:
- $5/8$ yard of White fabric
- $1/8$ yard (or fat quarters) each of Dot fabrics
  - Pale Pink, Pink, Pale Blue, Lavender, Aqua, Purple, Red, Brown
- $1/2$ yard of Turquoise dot fabric
- 1 yard of backing fabric
- 29" x 39" batting
- Embroidery floss - Pink, Blue, Lavender, Aqua, Purple, Turquoise, Red, Brown
- Assorted buttons - $5/32$" baby buttons
- One Red $3/4$" heart-shaped button
- pins • thread • needles • scissors

CUTTING:
- Cut twelve 7" squares of White fabric
- Cut twenty four $1^1/4$" x 7" strips of dot fabric
  (6 each of Pale Pink, Pink, Pale Blue, Lavender)
- Cut two $1^1/4$" x 32" strips of Aqua dot fabric
- Cut two $1^3/4$" x $23^1/2$" strips of Purple dot fabric
- Cut two $1^3/4$" x 32" strips of Purple dot fabric
- Cut two $3^1/4$" x $34^1/2$" of Turquoise dot fabric
- Cut two $3^1/4$" x 29" of Turquoise dot fabric
- Cut a 29" x 39" piece of quilt batting

TIP: Use $1/4$" seam allowances throughout.

continued on page 72

Patterns continued on pages 70-75

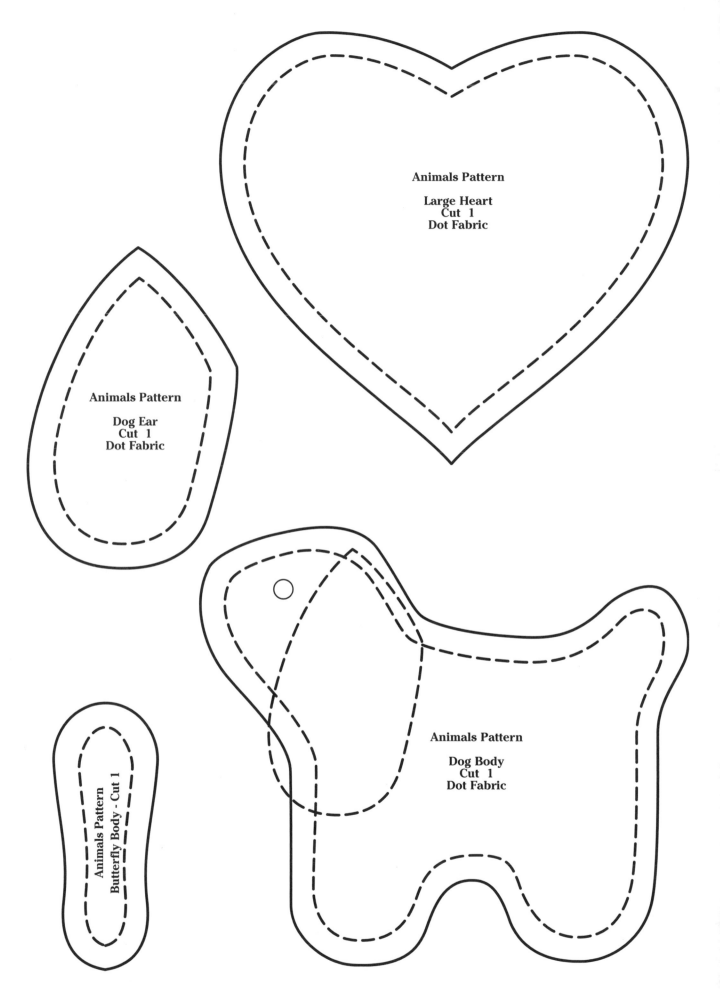

Animals Pattern

Large Heart
Cut 1
Dot Fabric

Animals Pattern

Dog Ear
Cut 1
Dot Fabric

Animals Pattern
Butterfly Body - Cut 1

Animals Pattern

Dog Body
Cut 1
Dot Fabric

Favorite Animals Quilt

continued from page 70

INSTRUCTIONS:

1. Lightly mark the placement of designs onto White fabric squares.

2. Cut all design parts from appropriate colors of dot fabric.

3. On applique piece, fold seams under $1/4$", press folded edges.

4. Pin each design in place. With the embroidery floss color of your choice, use a Blanket Stitch or Stem stitch around the edges and a Backstitch on all detail lines. Sew on buttons.

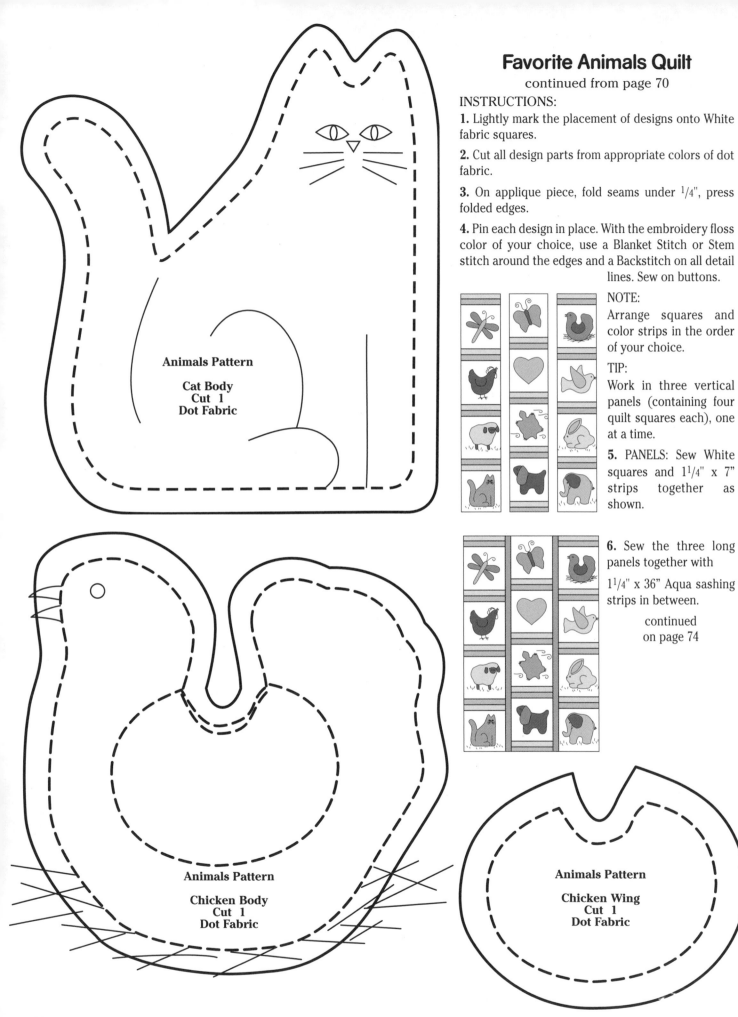

NOTE:
Arrange squares and color strips in the order of your choice.

TIP:
Work in three vertical panels (containing four quilt squares each), one at a time.

5. PANELS: Sew White squares and $1 1/4$" x 7" strips together as shown.

6. Sew the three long panels together with $1 1/4$" x 36" Aqua sashing strips in between.

continued on page 74

Animals Pattern

Cat Body
Cut 1
Dot Fabric

Animals Pattern

Chicken Body
Cut 1
Dot Fabric

Animals Pattern

Chicken Wing
Cut 1
Dot Fabric

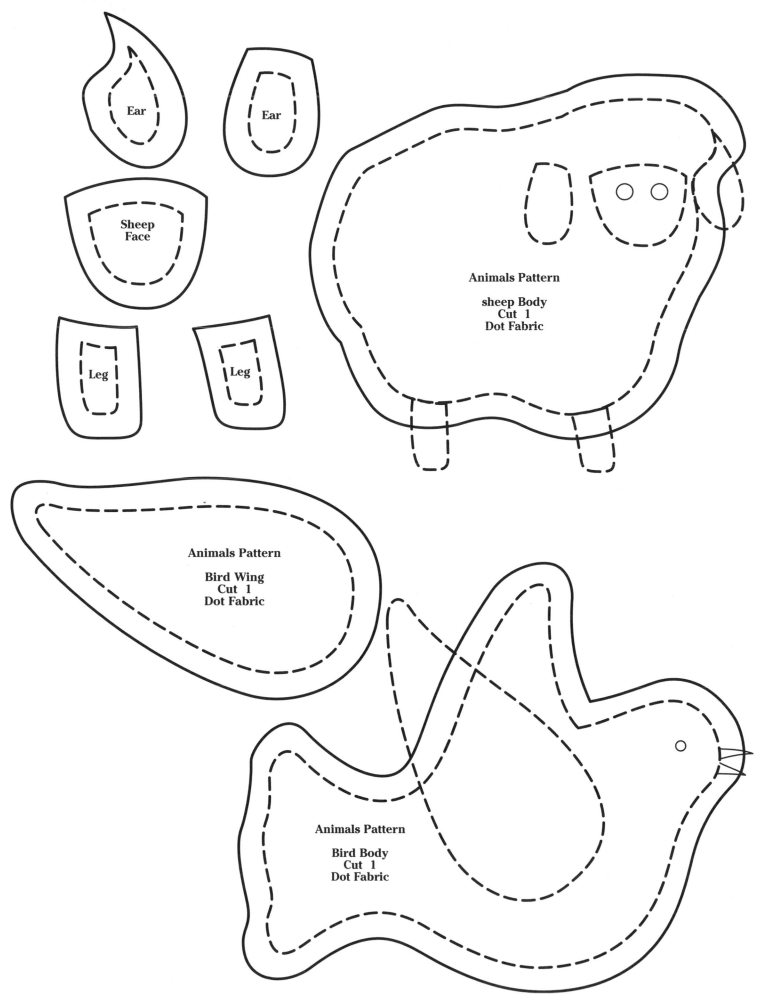

Ear

Ear

Sheep
Face

Leg

Leg

Animals Pattern

**sheep Body
Cut 1
Dot Fabric**

Animals Pattern

**Bird Wing
Cut 1
Dot Fabric**

Animals Pattern

**Bird Body
Cut 1
Dot Fabric**

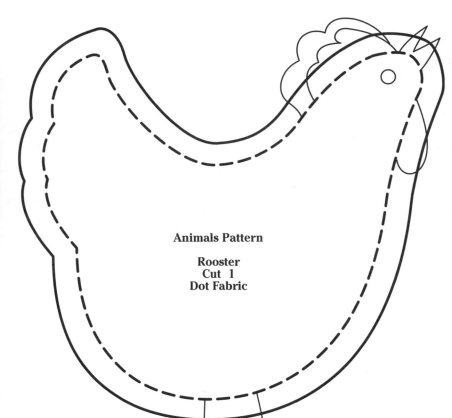

Animals Pattern

Rooster
Cut 1
Dot Fabric

Animals Quilt

continued from page 72

7. Sew $1^3/4"$ x 32" Purple sashing strips to quilt sides.

8. Sew $1^3/4"$ x $23^1/2"$ Purple sashing strips to top and bottom.

9. Sew $3^1/4"$ x 29" Turquoise sashing strips to left and right sides.

10. Sew $3^1/2"$ x 44" Turquoise sashing strips to top and bottom.

11. Sandwich batting between quilt top and backing fabric; pin in place.

12. Hand stitch bias binding around the edge of quilt.

13. Quilt in the ditch or quilt as desired.

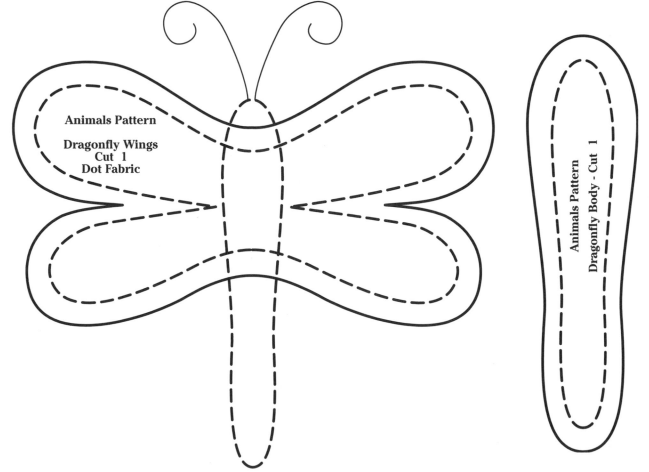

Animals Pattern

Dragonfly Wings
Cut 1
Dot Fabric

Animals Pattern
Dragonfly Body - Cut 1

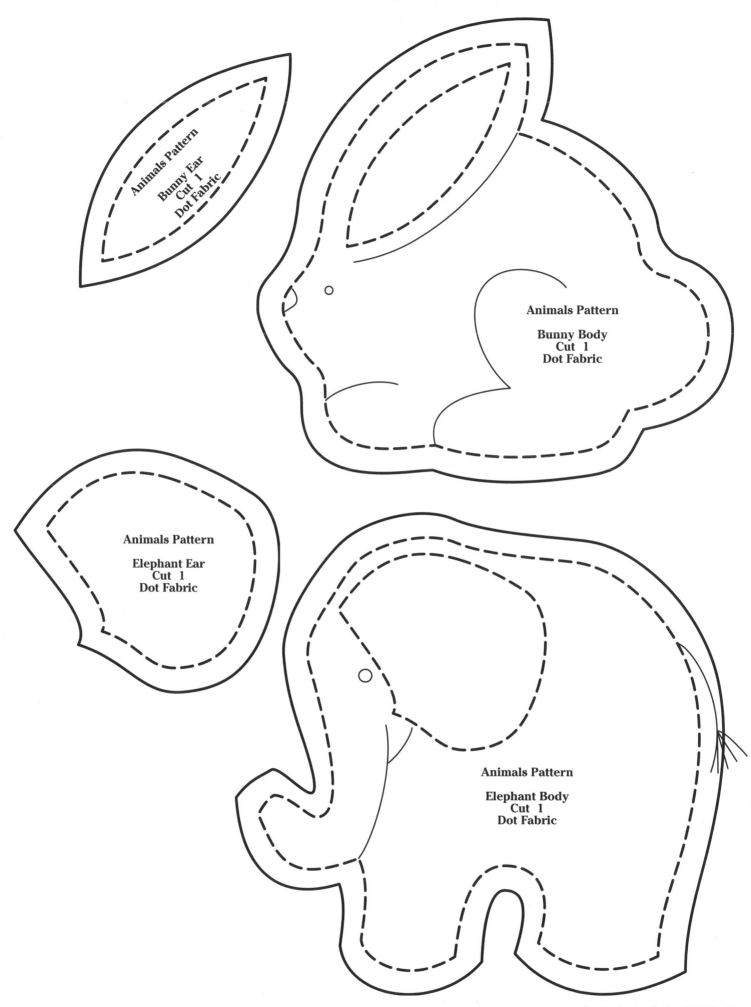

Animals Pattern

Bunny Ear
Cut 1
Dot Fabric

Animals Pattern

Bunny Body
Cut 1
Dot Fabric

Animals Pattern

Elephant Ear
Cut 1
Dot Fabric

Animals Pattern

Elephant Body
Cut 1
Dot Fabric

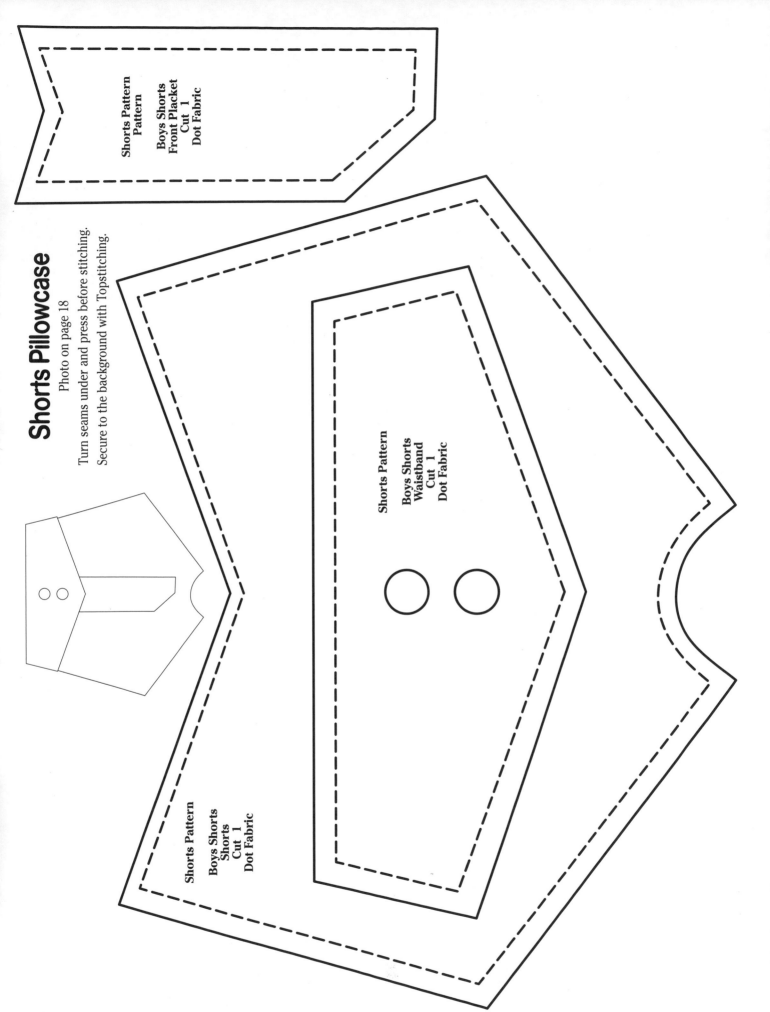

Shorts Pillowcase

Photo on page 18

Turn seams under and press before stitching.
Secure to the background with Topstitching.

Shorts Pattern Pattern

Boys Shorts
Front Placket
Cut 1
Dot Fabric

Shorts Pattern

Boys Shorts
Waistband
Cut 1
Dot Fabric

Shorts Pattern

Boys Shorts
Shorts
Cut 1
Dot Fabric

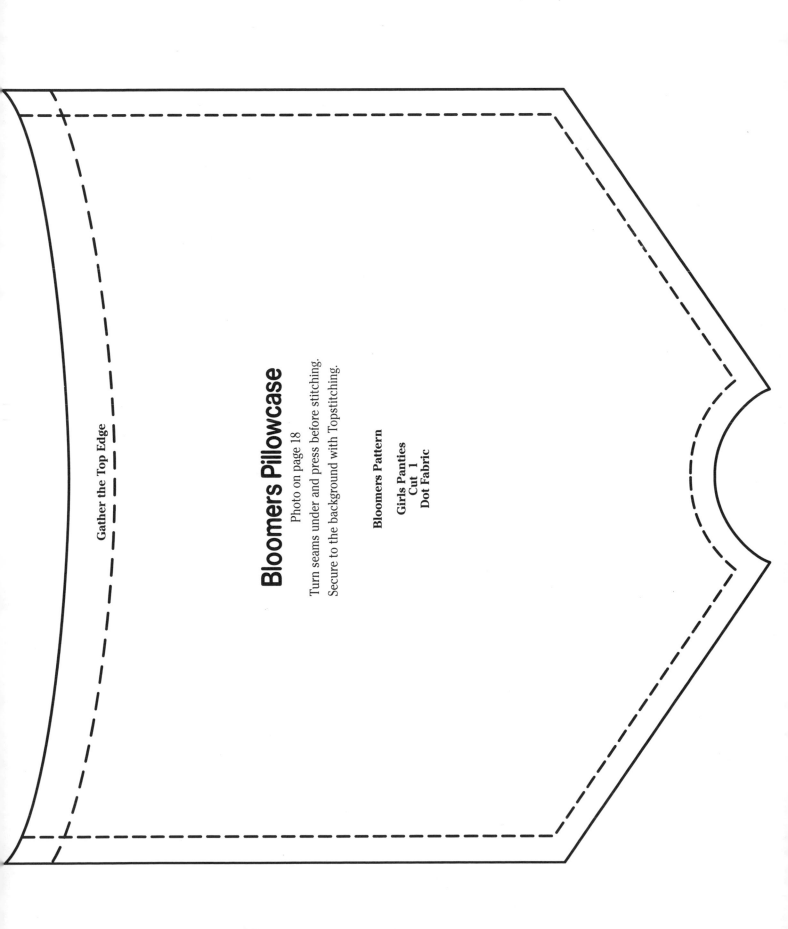

Gather the Top Edge

Bloomers Pillowcase

Photo on page 18

Turn seams under and press before stitching.
Secure to the background with Topstitching.

Bloomers Pattern

Girls Panties
Cut 1
Dot Fabric

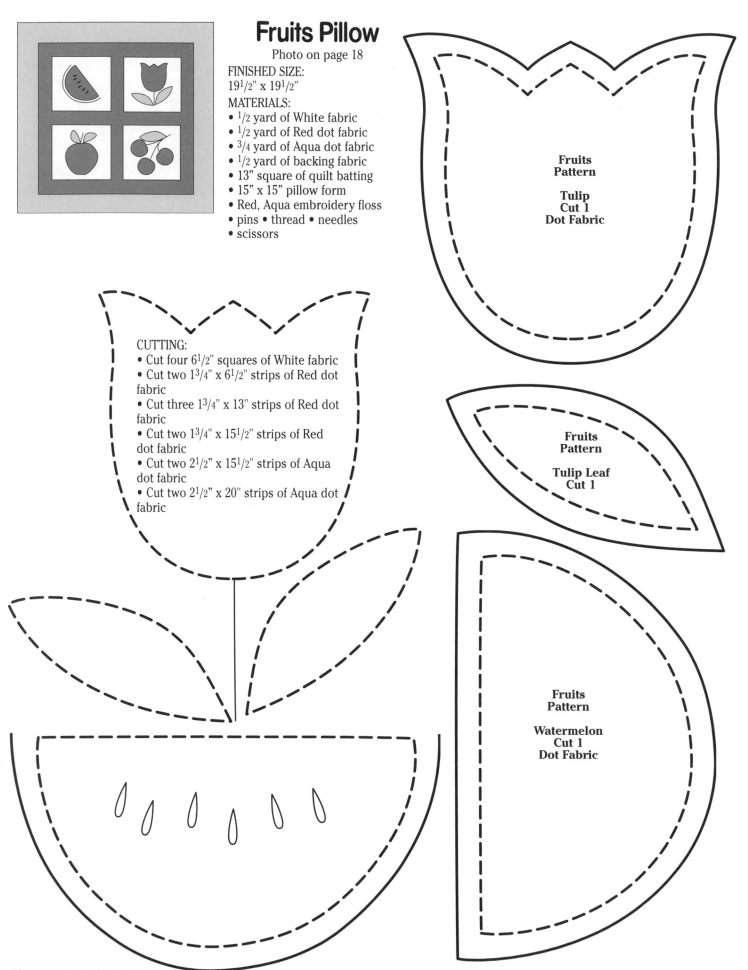

Fruits Pillow

Photo on page 18

FINISHED SIZE:
$19^{1}/_{2}$" x $19^{1}/_{2}$"

MATERIALS:
- $^{1}/_{2}$ yard of White fabric
- $^{1}/_{2}$ yard of Red dot fabric
- $^{3}/_{4}$ yard of Aqua dot fabric
- $^{1}/_{2}$ yard of backing fabric
- 13" square of quilt batting
- 15" x 15" pillow form
- Red, Aqua embroidery floss
- pins • thread • needles
- scissors

CUTTING:
- Cut four $6^{1}/_{2}$" squares of White fabric
- Cut two $1^{3}/_{4}$" x $6^{1}/_{2}$" strips of Red dot fabric
- Cut three $1^{3}/_{4}$" x 13" strips of Red dot fabric
- Cut two $1^{3}/_{4}$" x $15^{1}/_{2}$" strips of Red dot fabric
- Cut two $2^{1}/_{2}$" x $15^{1}/_{2}$" strips of Aqua dot fabric
- Cut two $2^{1}/_{2}$" x 20" strips of Aqua dot fabric

Fruits
Pattern

Tulip
Cut 1
Dot Fabric

Fruits
Pattern

Tulip Leaf
Cut 1

Fruits
Pattern

Watermelon
Cut 1
Dot Fabric

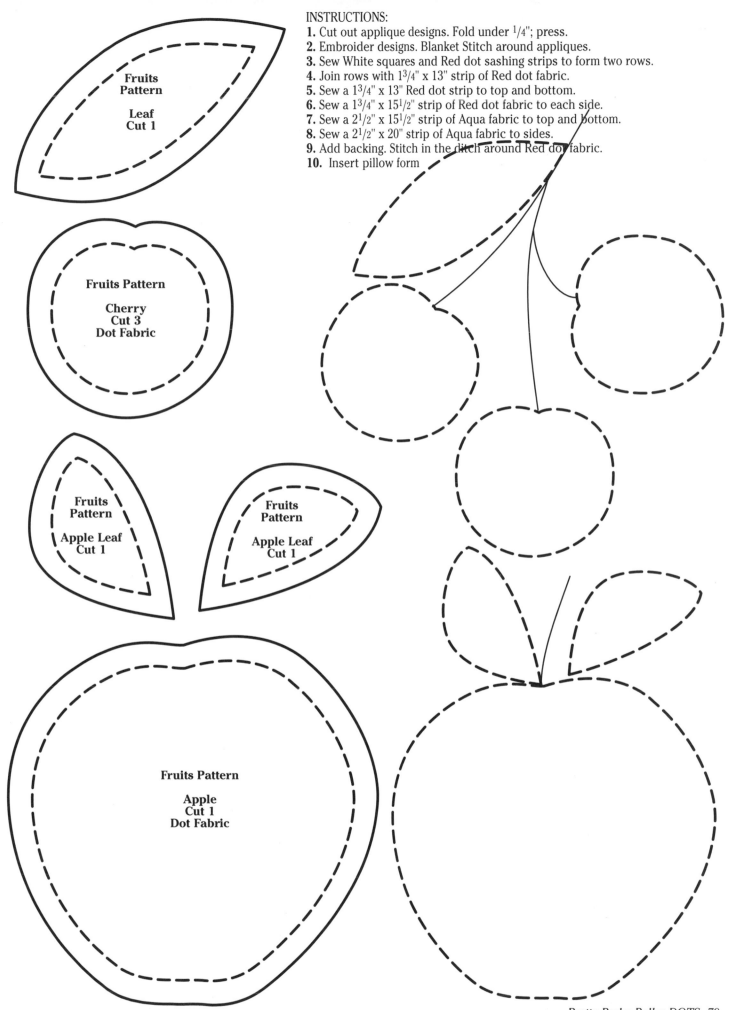

Fruits Pattern

Leaf
Cut 1

Fruits Pattern

Cherry
Cut 3
Dot Fabric

Fruits Pattern

Apple Leaf
Cut 1

Fruits Pattern

Apple Leaf
Cut 1

Fruits Pattern

Apple
Cut 1
Dot Fabric

INSTRUCTIONS:
1. Cut out applique designs. Fold under $^1/_4$"; press.
2. Embroider designs. Blanket Stitch around appliques.
3. Sew White squares and Red dot sashing strips to form two rows.
4. Join rows with $1^3/_4$" x 13" strip of Red dot fabric.
5. Sew a $1^3/_4$" x 13" Red dot strip to top and bottom.
6. Sew a $1^3/_4$" x $15^1/_2$" strip of Red dot fabric to each side.
7. Sew a $2^1/_2$" x $15^1/_2$" strip of Aqua fabric to top and bottom.
8. Sew a $2^1/_2$" x 20" strip of Aqua fabric to sides.
9. Add backing. Stitch in the ditch around Red dot fabric.
10. Insert pillow form

Months of the Year Quilt

Photo on page 15

FINISHED SIZE: 34" x 45"

TIPS: Use all cotton fabric. Use $1/4$" seams throughout. Quilting stitch in the ditch and circles.

MATERIALS:
- 1 yard of White fabric
- $1/6$ yard of 12 different colors of dot fabrics
- $1 1/3$ yards of backing fabric
- 3 yards of Black $3/8$" double fold bias binding
- Red, Blue, Green, Yellow, Black embroidery floss
- Six $7/8$" Black buttons
- Quilt batting
- pins • thread • needles • scissors

CUTTING:

TIP: Embroider blocks before cutting apart.
- Cut 12 White squares - each 8" x 8"
- Cut 24 strips $2 1/4$" x 8" (2 from each dot fabric)
- Cut 24 strips $2 1/4$" x $11 1/2$" (2 from each dot fabric)
- Cut one $34 1/4$" x $45 1/4$" piece of fabric for backing

INSTRUCTIONS:

1. Mark twelve 9" x 9" squares on the White fabric.

2. Trace one month design in the center of each White square.

3. Embroider design with an appropriate color of floss.

4. Cut squares apart. Cut the size of each square down to 8" x 8".

5. Choose one set of 2 1/4" wide dot strips for each month (coordinate with the color of floss).

6. Sew one 8" sashing strip to the left side of block; and one to the right side. Sew one 11" sashing strip to the top of block; and another one to the bottom. Repeat 11 more times to complete all blocks.

7. Sew blocks together into four strips with 3 blocks across in each.

8. Sew strips together to complete the quilt top.

9. Sandwich batting between quilt top and backing fabric; pin in place.

10. Hand stitch bias binding around the edge of quilt.

11. Quilt in the ditch or quilt as desired. Mark 3" diameter circles at the six 4-block intersections and quilt on those lines.

Optional: Sew buttons in the center of each circle.

Patterns continued on pages 82-89

Quilts are close to my heart!

February

March

Lucky Quilter!

Salute the Quilt

July

Months of the Year Quilt

Photo on page 99
Patterns continued on pages 80-89

Stitch an old saying,
Hang it up real high.
Read it every evening
And follow it - or try!

Months of the Year Quilt

Photo on page 99

Patterns continued on pages 80-89

May
Basket

September

June

Wedding Quilts

Months of the Year Quilt

Photo on page 99
Patterns continued on pages 80-89

Months of the Year Quilt

Photo on page 99
Patterns continued on pages 80-89

Give a Quilt

November

There is superstition about Polka Dots on
New Year's Eve...
"Wearing polka dots on New Year's Eve
brings lots of money in your pocket."
This folk belief originated in the Philippines.
Polka dots symbolize coins. By wearing polka dots, one
is drawing money to themselves. By wearing polka dots,
one will be entering the New Year wealthy since the
dots represent money that is to come.

"Piece" on Earth

December

Pink Peach

Photo on page 8

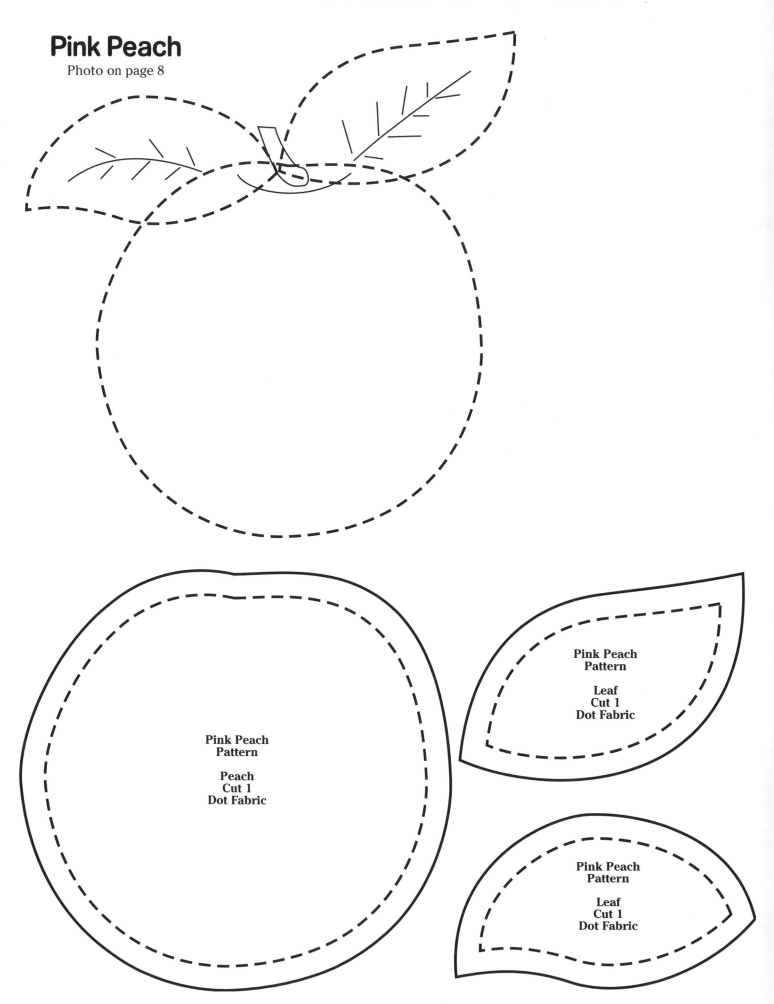

Pink Peach
Pattern

Peach
Cut 1
Dot Fabric

Pink Peach
Pattern

Leaf
Cut 1
Dot Fabric

Pink Peach
Pattern

Leaf
Cut 1
Dot Fabric

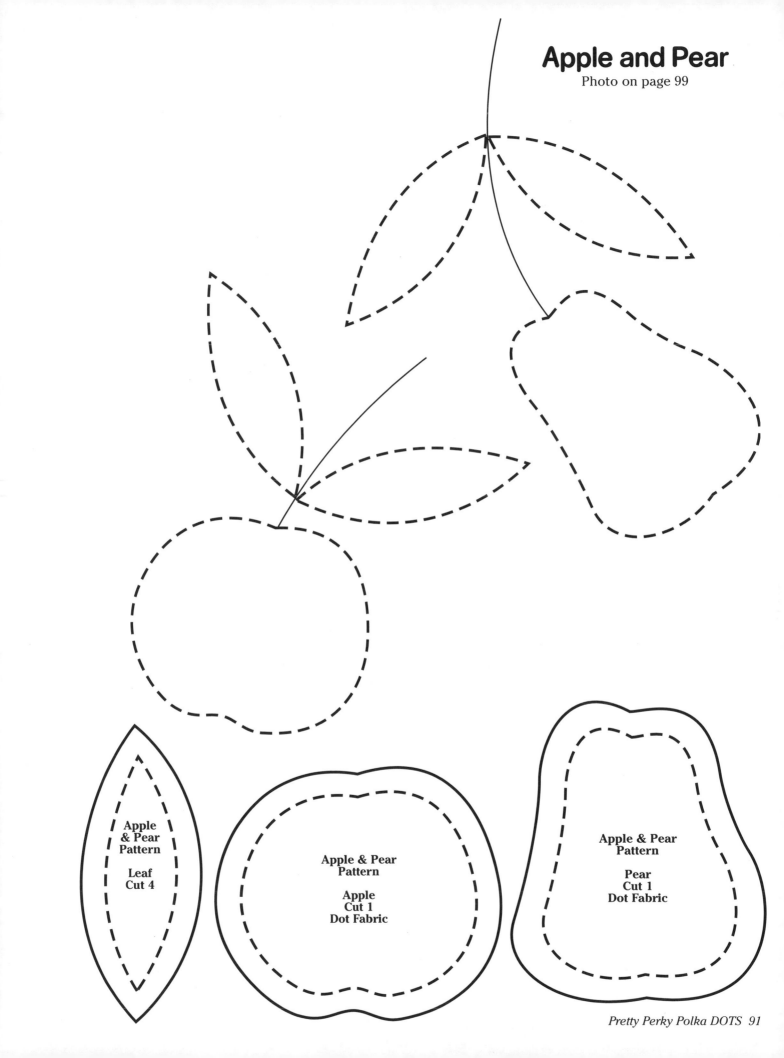

Apple and Pear

Photo on page 99

Apple & Pear Pattern

Leaf Cut 4

Apple & Pear Pattern

Apple Cut 1 Dot Fabric

Apple & Pear Pattern

Pear Cut 1 Dot Fabric

Boy and Girl

Boy Pattern

Photo on page 99

TIP: Add a ¼" seam to all applique patterns. Turn seams under and press before stitching. Secure to the background with a Blind Stitch.

Boy and Girl

Girl Pattern

Photo on page 99

TIP: Add a $1/4$" seam to all applique patterns. Turn seams under and press before stitching. Secure to the background with a Blind Stitch.

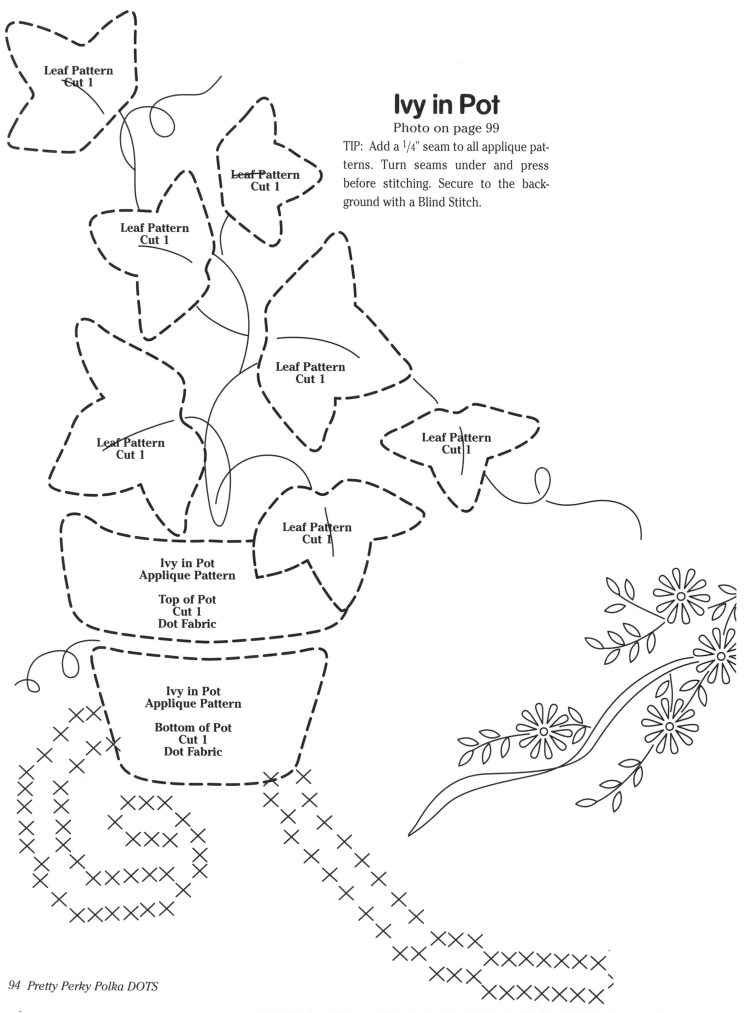

Leaf Pattern
Cut 1

Leaf Pattern
Cut 1

Leaf Pattern
Cut 1

Leaf Pattern
Cut 1

Leaf Pattern
Cut 1

Leaf Pattern
Cut 1

Leaf Pattern
Cut 1

Leaf Pattern
Cut 1

Ivy in Pot

Photo on page 99

TIP: Add a $\frac{1}{4}$" seam to all applique patterns. Turn seams under and press before stitching. Secure to the background with a Blind Stitch.

Ivy in Pot
Applique Pattern

Top of Pot
Cut 1
Dot Fabric

Ivy in Pot
Applique Pattern

Bottom of Pot
Cut 1
Dot Fabric

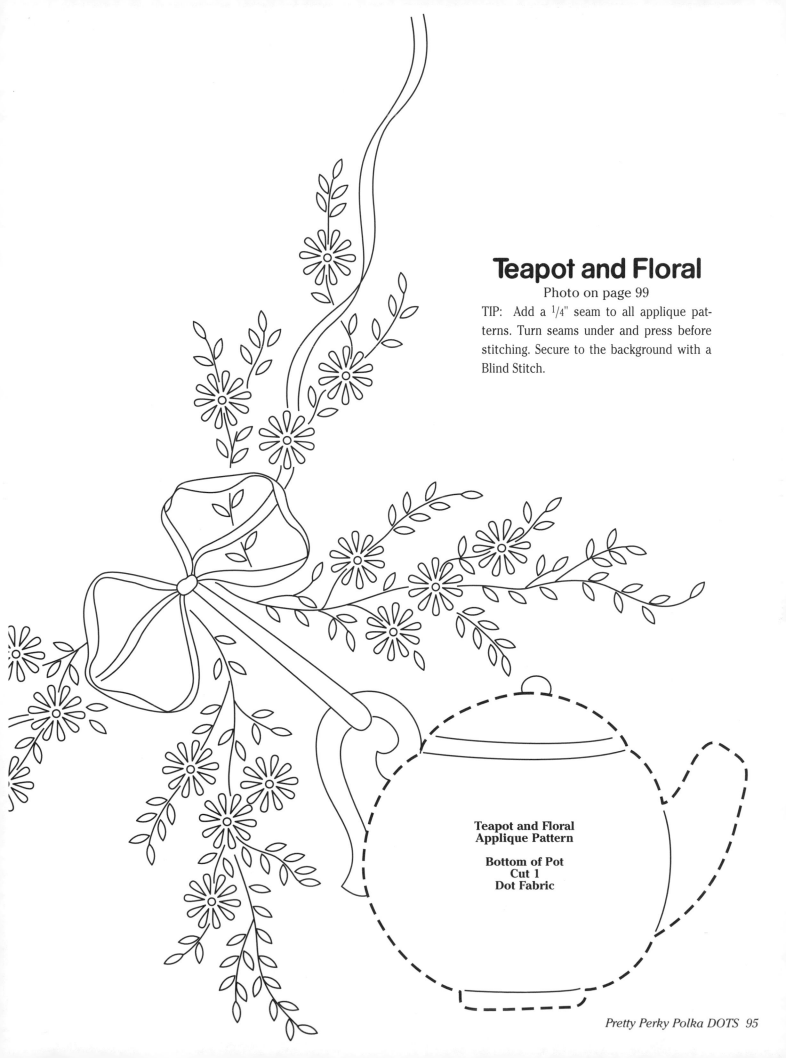

Teapot and Floral

Photo on page 99

TIP: Add a ¹/₄" seam to all applique patterns. Turn seams under and press before stitching. Secure to the background with a Blind Stitch.

Teapot and Floral
Applique Pattern

Bottom of Pot
Cut 1
Dot Fabric

Care of Linens

Washing -

- Test for colorfastness on the seam allowance. Let several drops of water fall through the fabric onto white blotter paper. If color appears, the fabric is not colorfast.
- To set dye, soak fabric in water and vinegar.
- Wash with a very mild detergent or soap, using tepid water. Follow all label instructions carefully.
- Do not use chlorine bleach on fine linen. Whiten it by hanging it in full sunlight.

Stain Removal -

- Grease - Use a presoak fabric treatment and wash in cold water.
- Nongreasy - Soak in cold water to neutralize the stain. Apply a presoak and then wash in cold water.
- Ballpoint Ink - Place on an absorbent material and soak with denatured or rubbing alcohol. Apply room temperature glycerin and flush with water. Finally, apply ammonia and quickly flush with water.
- Candle Wax - Place fabric between layers of absorbent paper and iron on low setting. Change paper as it absorbs wax. If a stain remains, wash with peroxide bleach.
- Rust - Remove with lemon juice, oxalic acid or hydrofluoric acid.

Storage -

- Wash and rinse thoroughly in soft water.
- Do not size or starch.
- Place cleaned linen on acid-free tissue paper and roll loosely.
- Line storage boxes with a layer of acid-free tissue paper.
- Place rolled linens in a box. Do not stack. Weight causes creases.
- Do not store linens in plastic bags.
- Hang linen clothing in a muslin bag or cover with a cotton sheet.

'Tinting' with Crayons

Crayons Aren't Paints - Even though ironing softens the crayon, their hard nature means that some of the texture of the fabric and the strokes you make will show through - just like when you make a rubbing over a penny. Making your strokes in the same direction can be challenging in large areas, which is why projects with smaller individual areas of color are best suited to crayon tinting.

Tip: Practice on extra muslin first.

Supplies - Muslin fabric, 24 colors of crayons (or more), embroidery floss, embroidery hoop, micron pen, needle

Crayon Hints - Besides being convenient, crayons come in beautiful colors and aren't intimidating. Simply color in the spaces to create the look you want.

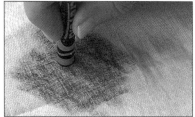

Build Up Color, Edges In

Add layers of crayon color with the strokes going in one direction, or opposite directions for a darker effect. Start lightly - you can always add more. Shading built up from the edges inward helps model or add depth to pieces, so that the tinted areas are not only colorful but three-dimensional as well. You can even choose to leave an area completely open to give a strong highlight.

Use the Correct End

For filling in color, the blunt end of the crayon works best and it works even better if its hard edge is rounded off a little before you start. Keep the pointed end for details or adding a fine shaded line to edges.

Tip: Let the Fabric Do the Work

A shaded fabric (white on white or off white) adds depth to your shading. Larger designs are a little better than fine ones because they give more variety.

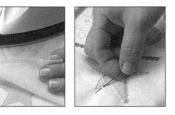

1. Position fabric over a pattern, secure corners with masking tape.

Trace pattern outline directly onto muslin with a blue-line water erase pen or a pencil.

2. Place fabric on a pad of extra fabric and color areas with regular children's crayons.

Color the pattern well with crayon color.

3. Sandwich the fabric between two sheets of plain paper.

Iron on 'cotton' setting to 'set' the crayon colors.

4. If desired, back design with another piece of fabric, place fabric or layers in an embroidery hoop.

Use 3-ply floss to outline the design.

Embroidery Stitches

Working with Floss. Separate embroidery floss.

Use 24" lengths of floss and a #8 embroidery needle.

Use 2 to 3 ply floss to outline large elements of the design and to embroider larger and more stylized patterns.

Use 2 ply for the small details on some items.

Blanket Stitch

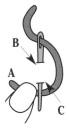

Come up at A, hold the thread down with your thumb, go down at B. Come back up at C with the needle tip over the thread. Pull the stitch into place. Repeat, outlining with the bottom legs of the stitch. Use this stitch to edge fabrics.

Chain Stitch

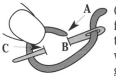

Come up at A. To form a loop, hold the thread down with your thumb, go down at B (as close as possible to A). Come back up at C with the needle tip over the thread. Repeat to form a chain.

Cross Stitch

Make a diagonal Straight stitch (up at A, down at B) from upper right to lower left. Come up at C and go down at D to make another diagonal Straight stitch the same length as the first one. The stitch will form an X.

French Knot

Come up at A. Wrap the floss around the needle 2 to 3 times. Insert the needle close to A. Hold the floss and pull the needle through the loops gently.

Herringbone Stitch

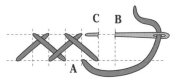

Come up at A. Make a slanted stitch to the top right, inserting the needle at B. Come up a short distance away at C.

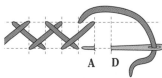

Insert the needle at D to complete the stitch. Bring the needle back up at the next A to begin a new stitch. Repeat.

Pay attention to backgrounds.

When working with lighter-colored fabrics, do not carry dark flosses across large unworked background areas. Stop and start again to prevent unsightly 'ghost strings' from showing through the front.

Another option is to back tinted muslin with another layer of muslin before you add embroidery stitches. This will help keep 'ghost strings' from showing.

Lazy Daisy Stitch

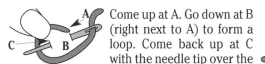 

Come up at A. Go down at B (right next to A) to form a loop. Come back up at C with the needle tip over the thread. Go down at D to make a small anchor stitch over the top of the loop.

Running Stitch

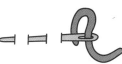

Come up at A. Weave the needle through the fabric, making short, even stitches. Use this stitch to gather fabrics, too.

Satin Stitch

Work small straight stitches close together and at the same angle to fill an area with stitches. Vary the length of the stitches as required to keep the outline of the area smooth.

Stem Stitch

Work from left to right to make regular, slanting stitches along the stitch line. Bring the needle up above the center of the last stitch. Also called 'Outline' stitch.

Straight Stitch

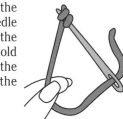

Come up at A and go down at B to form a simple flat stitch. Use this stitch for hair for animals and for simple petals on small flowers.

Whip Stitch

Insert the needle under a few fibers of one layer of fabric. Bring the needle up through the other layer of fabric. Use this stitch to attach the folded raw edges of fabric to the back of pieces or to attach bindings around the edges of quilts and coverlets.

Polka Dots

The sophistication of cotton fabric in the 1990's almost retired the dot. Unless used along with other designs, polka dots were considered too "quaint" for current trends.

As 2000 rolled around, the repeat of "what's old is new again" became popular everywhere. Bright bouncy colors hit fashions and quilt designs.

This is a perfect scenario for the "dot" to be popular again. The "retro" look hit in 2002 with the approval of a much younger generation. Fabric lovers are again responding to the cute and carefree look of the polka dot.

Dots are printed with other popular and fun motifs like cherries, scottie dogs, fruits, animals and teapots.

Designers know that in the past lies a clue to the future. A century later the dot has bounced back to get its due!

Ann W. Hazelwood

Patches Girls Rally for "Dots"

Just as in the success of Patches etc. (25 years) the success of any venture is not done alone.

Being surrounded by talented people makes it easy to fulfill one's vision. No matter what the topic, the Patches etc. staff rallies when there is a fun, exciting project in the wind. In hopes of not leaving anyone out, listed below are the many fine contributors: Hallye Bone, Donna Whitton, Wynema Bean, Karen Fornkahl, Norma Rennels, Bonnie Forscee, Sandra Staggs, Nancy Steele, Sharon Brader, Janet Thomlison, Joel Watkins IV and Marilyn Kempfer.

Every attempt has been made to obtain permission to reproduce materials protected by copyright or to use copyright free materials used in this book. Where omissions may have occurred, the producers will be happy to acknowledge this in future printings.

Strawberries
Photo on page 99

Strawberry Applique Pattern

**Cut 3
Red Polka Dot fabric**

TIP: Turn seams under and press before stitching. Secure to the background with a Blind Stitch.

At Home in the Kitchen

Delightful designs for Polka Dots grace pillows, tablecloths and towels.

Teapot
Pattern on page 95

Ivy in Pot
Pattern on page 94

Apple & Pear
Pattern on page 91

Boy & Girl
Pattern on page 92-93

Sunbonnet Girl
Pattern on page 59

Fun Fabrics of the 50s shown on page 2
published by Shiffer Publishing, Ltd., Atglen, PA

MANY THANKS to my friends for their cheerful help and wonderful ideas!
Kathy McMillan - Jen Tennyson
Barbara Worth - David & Donna Thomason
Marti Wyble - Charlie Davis Young
Mary Beth Kauffman - Janie Ray - Linda Rocamontes